Rape Myths, the Bible, and #MeToo

Biblical studies is increasingly interdisciplinary and frequently focuses on how the Bible is read, received, and represented in the contemporary world, including in politics, news media, and popular culture. *Rape Myths, the Bible, and #MeToo* illustrates this with particular and critical assessment of #MeToo and its rapid and global impact. Rape myths – in particular the myth that rape victims are complicit in the violence they encounter, which consequently renders sexual violence 'not so bad' – are examined both with regard to the current backlash to #MeToo and to biblical texts that undermine the violence perpetrated by rape. This includes aggressive media attacks on the accusers of powerful men, as well as depictions of biblical rape victims such as Dinah (Genesis 34), Bathsheba, and Tamar (2 Samuel 11–13). Biblical studies channels and expresses wider cultural and political manifestations. This exemplifies that the influence of ancient texts is abiding and the study of the past cutting edge.

Johanna Stiebert is Professor of Hebrew Bible at the University of Leeds, UK. Her two most recent monographs are *Fathers and Daughters in the Hebrew Bible* (2013) and *First-Degree Incest and the Hebrew Bible* (2016). She is co-director of The Shiloh Project.

Rape Culture, Religion and the Bible
Series Editors:
Katie Edwards
University of Sheffield, UK
Caroline Anne Blyth
University of Auckland, New Zealand
Johanna Stiebert
University of Leeds, UK

Rape Myths, the Bible, and #MeToo
Johanna Stiebert

For more information about this series, please visit: www.routledge.com/Rape-Culture-Religion-and-the-Bible/book-series/RCRB

Rape Myths, the Bible, and #MeToo

Johanna Stiebert

Routledge
Taylor & Francis Group

LONDON AND NEW YORK

First published 2020
by Routledge
2 Park Square, Milton Park, Abingdon, Oxon OX14 4RN

and by Routledge
52 Vanderbilt Avenue, New York, NY 10017

Routledge is an imprint of the Taylor & Francis Group, an informa business

British Library Cataloguing-in-Publication Data
A catalogue record for this book is available from the British Library

Library of Congress Cataloging-in-Publication Data
Names: Stiebert, Johanna, author.
Title: Rape myths, the Bible and #MeToo / Johanna Stiebert.
Description: Abingdon, Oxon ; New York : Routledge, 2020. |
Includes bibliographical references and index.
Identifiers: LCCN 2019035238 (print) | LCCN 2019035239
(ebook) | ISBN 9780367245184 (hardback) | ISBN
9780429282966 (ebook) | ISBN 9781000751826 (adobe pdf) |
ISBN 9781000752083 (epub) | ISBN 9781000751956 (mobi)
Subjects: LCSH: Bible. Old Testament–Criticism,
interpretation, etc. | Rape in the Bible. | Victims in the Bible. |
Rape–Religious aspects–Christianity. | Rape–Public opinion. |
Rape in mass media.
Classification: LCC BS1199.R27 S75 2020 (print) | LCC
BS1199.R27 (ebook) | DDC 220.8/3641532–dc23
LC record available at https://lccn.loc.gov/2019035238
LC ebook record available at https://lccn.loc.gov/2019035239

ISBN: 978-0-367-24518-4 (hbk)
ISBN: 978-0-429-28296-6 (ebk)

Typeset in Bembo
by Wearset Ltd, Boldon, Tyne and Wear

MIX
Paper from
responsible sources
FSC
www.fsc.org   FSC® C013985

Printed in the United Kingdom
by Henry Ling Limited

This book is for my inspirational sister Viki (aka Schnutzi) who has always looked out for me

Contents

Acknowledgements

I would like to thank the Arts and Humanities Research Council and the Global Challenges Research Fund for providing generous financial support for ongoing projects aimed at actively resisting gender-based violence in the UK, southern Africa, and New Zealand. Other funding for smaller subsidiary projects that have also informed and inspired this book has come from the White Rose Consortium, the Worldwide Universities Network, and the British Academy.

At the source of this volume and of the series to which it belongs is the Shiloh Project. This project was initiated in early 2017 to explore the intersections of rape culture, religion, and the Bible. The project promotes activism for gender justice, interdisciplinary research, and artistic expression, collaboration, and the sharing of resources. It has brought me into what I can best describe as purposeful friendship with my wonderful co-directors and co-editors, Caroline and Katie. Working with both of you has been the highlight of my many years in universities. The Shiloh Project has also brought us into collaboration with extraordinary individuals and organisations from all over the world. A shout out especially to Legabibo of Botswana and the Talitha Qumi Institute of Ghana.

I also want to thank my colleagues at the University of Leeds and my fabulous family. While I take full responsibility for any errors or weaknesses in this volume, I could not have done this without you. Especial thanks go to 'Drummond and Desmond' (you know who you are).

Introduction

At the outset

This book focuses on biblical texts that depict sexual violence and on how contemporary conversations about sexual violence, sexual harassment, and #MeToo can be engaged when reading and interpreting these texts. Particular focus is placed on the feature and function of rape myths: that is, stereotyped and prejudicial falsehoods about rape, rapists, and rape victims,[1] which help to underpin rape culture. In terms of approach, therefore, the book adopts a bifocal reading strategy, with one eye on ancient texts and the other on contemporary contexts, particularly popular media contexts. This approach has become increasingly popular in biblical studies over recent decades.

The book is in two main parts. Following some caveats and after delineating my use of the word 'rape', the first chapter examines two main thematic components: (1) the #MeToo movement and its abiding influence; and (2) depictions of sexual violence in biblical texts.

The second chapter then explores how the two elements can be brought together. It includes an overview of the concepts of rape culture and rape myth and details how these concepts function in the present, as well as with reference to texts in the Bible.

The conclusion summarizes what can be gained through a nuanced reading of biblical texts alongside contemporary events and publications that engage with #MeToo. Such a reading represents a form of acutely timely feminist advocacy, because understanding and then detoxifying the power dynamics in, and influence of, biblical texts plays a part in dismantling rape cultures.

Rape

Because much of the discussion that follows is about sexual violence – most centrally, rape – it is important, at the outset, if only briefly, to demarcate the term 'rape', both in the context of the Bible and in contemporary Anglophone usage.

The English word 'rape' derives from the Latin *raptio* ('abduction') and *rapere* ('to seize, carry off by force') and its meaning has shifted over time. The archaic use of 'rape' refers to the seizure of a person (most often a woman and for the purpose of sexual intercourse) – as in 'The Rape of Helen', the story that precipitates events recounted in the *Iliad*. Removal, or theft,[2] of a person – most frequently from the sphere of protection of either the natal or spousal family – not the consent of the person, was determinative of *raptio*, as well as of 'rape' in this usage. With Helen, for instance, the fact that Paris of Troy takes her away from her husband, Menelaus of Sparta, is what constitutes the *rape* of Helen. The absence of Menelaus's (not Helen's) consent is what counts. (That she is widely known as 'Helen of Troy' indicates how firmly associated she becomes with the place to which she is taken.) According to some versions, Helen goes willingly, that is, she consents (at least, to being taken). In modern understanding of the word such would not, consequently, qualify as rape (providing Helen was of age).[3] Nowadays, 'rape' pertains most often to the sexual and penetrative assault of a person against that person's will, with consent being a significant determinative factor.[4]

In contemporary Anglophone democracies some differences exist in terms of how rape is defined in law, with some specifying penile penetration of the vagina (envisaging or presuming specifically male–female rape),[5] while others include also penetration by digits or objects, as well as oral or anal penetration.[6] Most of these definitions, however, start from the point of view of non-consent (Popova 2019: 29–31). In British law, for instance, rape occurs 'when one person penetrates another with their penis without the consent of the person being penetrated' (*Sexual Offences Act 2003*). Moreover, the penetrator has to 'not reasonably believe [the person penetrated] consents' in order for a crime to qualify as rape (*Sexual Offences Act 2003*). The gender of the rape victim is not specified in law, but the perpetrator has a penis and is, consequently, presumed to be male. If a victim is forcefully penetrated with an object, the crime is not classed as rape in British law but as 'assault by penetration'.[7] In such a scenario, both perpetrator and victim can be of any gender. Crucial to these definitions of rape and assault is consent – that is, whether there is voluntary agreement to penetration by the one who is penetrated. If a person does not or cannot give consent – which may be on account of being too young (i.e. below the age of consent),[8] or mentally impaired,[9] or intoxicated, or unconscious, or under threat or duress, for instance – and that person is penetrated, rape has occurred.

The above paragraphs illustrate some of the complexities involved in defining rape, and that rape is an act that has multiple meanings, depending on the cultural and historical contexts in which it occurs. This has led some writers and scholars to challenge claims about the ubiquity of rape and the presence of rape cultures. Luke Gittos, for example, contests UK Office for National Statistics rape figures[10] in order to claim that rape is much more rare than these figures, as well as the media, feminists, rape support groups, and even rape victims, assert (Gittos 2015: 23–25). He does so by claiming that sexual dynamics and consent are extremely complicated and that those charged with rape often do not reasonably believe that the person they are accused of raping has not consented.[11]

I acknowledge that accurate rape statistics are difficult to obtain – given that rape most often takes place in a private setting with no witnesses or other monitoring (e.g. CCTV). Moreover, and for a combination of reasons including emotional and psychological ones, rape is likely to be significantly under-reported and, when it is reported, few cases end up in court and even fewer lead to a conviction. These are widely observed patterns and suggest *(pace* Gittos) that rape is a scourge and that statistics such as those for England and Wales – an estimated 85,000 rapes of women and 12,000 rapes of men in one year (Ministry of Justice, Home Office, and the Office for National Statistics 2013) – while very high, are possibly conservative.[12]

In this book 'rape' refers to penetrative sex without the consent of the penetrated party (i.e. the rape victim or rape survivor).[13] In the majority of cases discussed in this book men are the perpetrators of rape and the victims of rape are female.[14] This is because, as attested by the statistics cited above, by #MeToo revelations and media coverage, and by the Bible (all of which are my focus here) cases of the rape of women by men predominate. I acknowledge the many exceptions to this dominant pattern. My focus on the rape of women by men neither denies the existence of other dynamics of gendered violence, nor that the trauma and suffering endured by victims of such violence is any less profound. Indeed, female–male and male–male sexual exploitation are both likely to be even more under-reported than incidences of male–female sexual exploitation (see Cook-Daniels 2008; Javaid 2018). To give one indication of this, at the time of writing, a report conducted in 40 countries by the Economist Intelligence Unit (2019) revealed that sexually abused boys are being failed worldwide, not least because laws protecting children from sexual abuse are often worded to focus on the experiences of girls. This is further compounded by a tendency for support services (including shelters and legal aid) to be geared towards girls and women only. Moreover, social stigma, macho stereotypes, and homophobia further contribute to boys not reporting abuse. Without question, this subject and others, too, demand a platform.[15]

Coming back to framing rape in terms of consent: it is indeed the case that consent is complex insofar as it is not only about what happens between two individuals but is also 'enmeshed in social structures, cultural practices, and complex operations of power' (Popova 2019: 10). Consent is not, however, ambiguous or complicated in the vast majority of cases of rape.[16] Rapists are often well aware that their victim is not consenting. Asserting dominance and persisting where willingness is absent are part of the *raison d'être* of rape. As has been widely documented, rape, particularly in but not confined to feminist sources, is a crime of power and violence, calculated to express control and inflict fear and pain.[17] In her seminal early monograph on rape, *Against Our Will: Men, Women and Rape* (1975), Susan Brownmiller amply demonstrates that not only in settings of war but also in her own everyday US context, rape constitutes a conscious instrument of intimidation and of instilling and perpetuating fear.[18] Brownmiller also makes plain another now widely accepted point about rape: namely, that the consequence of rape is profound harm of multiple kinds to the victim. Alongside possible physical harm and damage, it is also psychological and emotional and often far-reaching and of a long-term nature. Again, this has been amply demonstrated in research from a range of disciplines, including clinical studies.[19] Much of this book seeks to dispel the counter-case, or rape myth, that rape is not really that bad.

This book does not offer an ethnographically-based investigation.[20] It is not written in collaboration with, and it offers no unfiltered insights from, persons who have disclosed sexual violence. I am aware of and admire scholars who do undertake such collaborations responsibly, respectfully, and sensitively; above all, because working alongside victims of sexual violence, particularly victims from groups that are disproportionately vulnerable to and scourged by rape (such as refugees, women living in poverty, certain ethnic and religious minorities, persons with disabilities, and sex workers, among others) counteracts their silencing and marginalization.[21] Such a book is not for me to write at this time.[22]

Rape and the Bible

Numerous commentators have pointed out that there is no Biblical Hebrew word that captures either the noun 'rape' or the verb 'to rape'[23] in terms of how these words are most often[24] used in modern English.

Nevertheless, the word appears widely and, in my view, legitimately in modern English translations of the Bible. To give one example, numerous translations of Genesis 34:2 use the English verb 'rape' to describe Shechem's action perpetrated against Dinah. Shechem is the subject of three Hebrew verbs: *wayyiqqach* ('he took'),[25] *wayyishkav* ('and he lay/ had sex [with]') and *way'annehâ* ('and he raped/denigrated her').[26] As I will argue, the third verb, from the root *'nh*,[27] regularly pertains to rape or to the profound denigration associated with rape in particular. The New International Version, the New Living Translation, the Christian Standard Bible, the Contemporary English Version, the Good News Translation, the Holman Christian Standard Bible, and God's Word Translation all use the English verb 'rape' at Genesis 34:2. Similarly, the New American Standard, the New Received Standard Version, the Berean and the Jewish Study Bible have the semantic equivalent, '[he] lay with her by force', and the New English Translation Bible, '[he] sexually assaulted her'. There are other translations,[28] but it is still significant that the verb 'to rape' is widely – and I would say appropriately – used, because the violence of Shechem's action and the absence (and unlikeliness) of Dinah's consent are understood.[29]

For some biblical scholars, however, the use of the word 'rape' in biblical translations is problematic, if not inaccurate. For example, Ellen Van Wolde carries out a full analysis of the Hebrew verbal root *'nh*, arguing that the translation 'rape' is 'not acceptable' (Van Wolde 2002a: 543) in *any* instance including in stories such as Genesis 34, Judges 19, and 2 Samuel 13, which are widely acknowledged as rape texts,[30] and which all include occurrences of *'innâ*, a *piel* stem form of *'nh*, with a woman as grammatical object.[31] I find the contortions of Van Wolde's argument, according to which *'innâ* repeatedly pertains to a man who has sex with a woman and debases her but without this *ever* being descriptive of rape, unconvincing. Van Wolde argues that the basic meaning of the root *'nh* is spatial and pertains to 'causative movement downwards' (Van Wolde 2002a: 530). Most often, she continues, this downward movement indicates a decline in a woman's social status, because *'nh* 'is an evaluative term used in a judicial context which marks a debasement of the social status of a woman with effects on the debasement of the men related to her within the whole social structure of Israelite society' (Van Wolde 2002a: 537; cf. Frymer-Kensky 1998[32]).

Speaking of Amnon's incestuous rape of Tamar (2 Samuel 13), Van Wolde also prefers to say that *'nh* 'refers to the purely physical and spatial act of pressing down' (Van Wolde 2002a: 543). But in this account both Amnon's force and Tamar's resistance are explicit. In respect of the Levite of Judges 19 who calls the Israelites to war by sending the body parts of his dismembered wife who was raped to death by a gang of thugs at Gibeah, Van Wolde (2002a: 539) again maintains that the Levite uses *'nh* 'not … to describe the act of the sexual abuse or rape itself. On the contrary, it is an evaluative term referring to complete annihilation'. The avoidance of the designation 'rape' once again strikes me here as peculiar. I find Van Wolde's (2002a: 541) claim that *'nh* does not ever refer to the sexual deed itself but, rather, to 'its consequences: the social debasement of the woman in the perspective of a social-judicial context' (Van Wolde 2002a: 542) unpersuasive – because the act of rape and its effect on the victim are rather difficult to separate in many cases.

While Hebrew *'nh* does not at every occurrence in the Hebrew Bible refer to forced sexual penetration (see Ullendorff 1978: 436), I would say that there is ample literary evidence to suggest it denotes rape in a number of instances. Among these are Genesis 34:2, Judges 19:24 and 20:5, 2 Samuel 13:12, 14, 22, and 32, and Lamentations 5:11. Sexual violence and force are clear in all of these examples: Dinah is taken, the Levite's concubine is killed, Tamar is seized and traumatized, and the women of Zion are violated as part of a brutal campaign of military conquest. Moreover, in other instances where piel *'nh* refers primarily or more precisely to denigration, or humbling, it is the association of the word with rape that expresses the profundity of affliction (e.g. Deuteronomy 8:2–3; Job 37:23). As Sandie Gravett notes,

> even though the cultures which wrote and passed down the … Bible conceived of sexual assault differently from our own, 'rape' remains the primary term we use in English for such violence. 'Rape' … communicates best on a bodily or visceral level to a twenty-first century reader, conveying the same feeling of forcible violation.
>
> (Gravett 2004: 297)

Alongside Van Wolde, other biblical commentators, too, argue against the use of the translation 'rape' for most, even all, biblical passages but give reasons other than philological ones. Robert Kawashima (2011), for example, suggests that because the contexts reflected in biblical texts do not depict women as empowered subjects, women's ability to give consent is impossible. In other words, if consent is a moot point, then so is rape.[33] This is, essentially, a culturally relativist argument of the 'those were different days' and 'that was "the way" back then' variety.

In a similar vein to Kawashima, Leah Rediger Schulte argues that it is an anachronism to speak of rape in antiquity:

> The majority of past scholarship on rape in the Bible applies a modern understanding of rape to biblical texts. While this has been done with either unintended modern bias or the best of intentions (to offer religious support for rape victims, for instance), biblical scholars must have a definition of biblical rape *qua* biblical rape in order to engage its meaning in an ancient context.
>
> (Schulte 2017: 10; cf. Yamada 2008: 4)

Schulte's statement suggests that it is possible to access the 'real' or 'original' meaning of 'biblical rape'.[34] I would contest this. Moreover, charges of anachronism in biblical studies are very often made by commentators who stress so-called 'objectivity',[35] and usually with regard to something they malign.[36]

While I am not contesting that there are vast differences in terms of customs, practices, values, and attitudes between the past (sometimes nebulously referred to as 'biblical times') and my own present, I see some degree of danger in the rape-erasing arguments detailed above. If we do not call the action committed against a person described in the biblical texts 'rape', even when the perpetrator's force is clear or highly likely and the victim's consent, even if this is not explicitly recorded, extremely unlikely, then it is much easier to claim or, at least, to suggest, that the effect was also not as traumatic.[37] By not using the word 'rape', the violence, absence of consent, and traumatic consequences attending rape are all easier to suppress. I am arguing instead – to paraphrase June Jordan – that language needs to be accountable to experience.[38] Moreover, because the Bible continues to exert influence into the present, erasure of rape from the Bible can enable the easier perpetuation of rape myths (e.g. the notion that rape is little more than 'just' sex). And rape myths, as this book will go on to demonstrate, have bearing and a damaging impact on real lives.

Granted, there is no explicit reference to or word for 'consent' in the Bible and no indication of anything like an age of consent[39] – but there is plenty of indication of what we would today call rape and I have no hesitation in calling it by that name. In this I align myself with feminist commentators such as Susanne Scholz (2005) and Caroline Blyth (2010)[40] who resist the impossibility of examining rape in biblical texts. This is, first, because I agree with them that objectivity in biblical interpretation is impossible. The only context in and from which I can read and interpret any biblical text is my own, and my reading is invariably shaped by my identities and experiences. This pertains to all interpreters and dictates that some degree of subjectivity is inevitable. This can also legitimate, I believe, a synergetic and bifocal endeavour such as mine here, of reading and interpreting sexual violence and rape myths in biblical texts alongside media reporting in my own time. Meaning is created and recreated in the place and at the time of interpretation and comes about through a fusion of ancient text and present context. A second reason for identifying and naming rape in biblical texts is because interpretive strategies that assert objectivity and thereby erase or neutralize a topic such as sexual violence detract from the urgency of confronting, resisting, and eliminating sexual violence. As Scholz (2005: 36.2) states, 'it is crucial to uplift ancient rape legislation and to identify past and present strategies that continue obfuscating the prevalence of rape even today.'

There are different words for and ways to describe rape in English, in Hebrew,[41] and in other languages also. The meaning of 'rape' in English and since 'biblical times' may have shifted, but my focus will not be on diachronic semantic developments. I will use the biblical text synchronically and apply the word 'rape' throughout to refer to depictions of forced penetration without the penetrated person's consent.

Given the abiding influence of the Bible, including as a text of authority, as well as the persistent presence of sexual violence, I see value, even urgency, in exploring rape in the Bible alongside the #MeToo present. As Blyth (2010: 7) notes, biblical texts not only 'reflect the ideologies, values, and assumptions of the community in which they are written; they also have the potential to validate and endorse these same ideologies, values, and assumptions within the communities in which they are read'. I agree that 'we should not underestimate the role that the scriptural traditions ... have played in *perpetuating* ... inequality ... up to the present day' (Blyth 2010: 16–17, italics in original). Moreover, we should not underestimate either the importance of fully investigating sexual violence in our own time because, in the words of Mithu Sanyal, '[r]ape informs our mental maps ... [and] the information we get about rape isn't just information about rape; it's also about gender, the relationship of the sexes to each other, and even sexuality' (Sanyal 2019: 1). I hope that the critical interfacing of biblical texts and #MeToo revelations can harness some of the movement's momentum and play a part in disrupting the perpetuation of rape myths.

Notes

1 See Note 13.

2 The notion of theft is also clear in Middle English *rapen, rappen,* 'to abduct, snatch' (cf. also German *Raub,* 'robbery'; see Sanyal 2019: 41).

3 On statutory rape and age of consent, see Note 8 below.

4 Schroeder explains that in Roman law and society *raptus* pertained to 'the crime of abduction, seizure, or theft of a person or property' and 'might or might not include sexual assault'. The designation that is closer in meaning to the current usage of the English noun rape is, *stuprum per vim,* 'defilement by force' (Schroeder 2007: 5).

5 This was the case in Botswana, although the law was amended in 1998 to move away from being either phallus- or gender-specific (see Government of the Republic of Botswana 1998). Sanyal (2019: 7, 125, 204) points out that the US Federal Bureau of Investigation defined a rape victim as female right up until 2012 or 2013. In Swiss law this remains the case. Sanyal (2019: 7–8) concludes, 'rape is the most gendered of all crimes. It's also the crime that genders us the most.'

6 On the Steubenville case and Ohio state law, according to which non-consensual digital penetration of the vagina constitutes rape, see Phillips (2017: 45). The US federal definition of rape also specifies 'the penetration, no matter how slight, of the vagina or anus with any body part or object, or oral penetration by a sex organ of another person, without the consent of the victim' (Popova 2019: 30).

7 See *Sexual Offences Act 2003.*

8 Sex with someone who, while consenting to sex, is either below the age of consent (an age that varies between different jurisdictions), or mentally handicapped, or otherwise not legally considered mentally capable of consenting to sexual activity, is in some legal systems designated statutory rape. Statutory rape usually refers to the crime of adults engaging in sexual activity with minors. The age of consent in the UK is 16. The age of gay consent was brought down from 18 to 16 in 2001. For a recent reconsideration of the age of consent in the UK, see Williams (2019).

9 At the time of writing, a case has recently been brought before the court of protection in London regarding a woman with mental impairment and her husband, to whom she has been married for 20 years. The case centred on whether the woman was still able to give consent to sex. The judge in the case, Mr Justice Hayden, commented that prohibiting sex could lead to a situation where the husband could face charges of rape and also that such an order would be difficult to police. Most controversially, he made the comment, 'I cannot think of any more obviously fundamental human right of a man to have sex with his wife' – which, understandably, met with some outrage (Bowcott 2019).

10 Gittos cites the crime survey of 2013. There has been a rise in sexual offences since (see Office for National Statistics 2018).

11 I have contested this elsewhere (Stiebert 2017, 2018).

12 For further details, see Rape Crisis England & Wales (No date).

13 Both designations, 'victim' and 'survivor' (of sexual harassment or abuse), are potentially problematic. The former focuses on the receiver of sexual assault as someone who has had something dreadful done to them and,

arguably, accentuates object status and passivity. On the other hand, 'victim' does acknowledge and emphasize the dreadfulness of what was perpetrated as well as lack of blame. 'Survivor', it could be said, confers more agency than 'victim' and focuses on overcoming the assault. 'Victim' may elicit protectiveness and 'survivor' admiration. For a fuller discussion see RAINN (No date).

14 I have simplified matters here. Mendes *et al.* (2019; 4, italics as in original) are correct in stating that sexual violence is not only heavily gendered but that those 'occupying *feminized bodies* [bear] the brunt of sexism *as well as homophobic, transphobic, and other forms of hate*'. It is correct that not only women and girls, including trans-women, but also males deemed to be effeminate, are at particular risk of rape.

15 Female–female sexual exploitation is likely to be the most rare and is certainly the least well documented (see Sjoberg 2016). Again, it is no less dreadful for being rare.

16 For a succinct, accessible, and thorough investigation of consent and the negotiation of respect for the bodily autonomy of another human being, see Popova (2019).

17 See Filipovic 2013.

18 Brownmiller's book has been enormously influential. Scholz (2018: 181) calls it '[t]he cornerstone publication that propelled feminists to openly address the problem of sexual violence'. Brownmiller has also been vociferously criticized, including for failure to address adequately intersectional, particularly racial, dimensions of sexual violence (see Davis 1981: 195–98; Sanyal 2019: 22–35, 86–87).

19 See, for example, Institut national de santé publique du Québec (No date) and Kilpatrick *et al.* (1981). The latter affirms feminist claims through quantitative clinical research. As I will discuss below, this general assertion does not dispute the fact that there exists a wide range of responses to rape and that victims of rape recover and heal, or not, in a diversity of ways.

20 One moving autoethnographic interpretation of rape is that by Moyo (2017), a survivor of rape, reflecting on Judges 19 during a visit to the Murambi Genocide Museum in Rwanda.

21 I am thinking here, for instance, of the collaborative work of the Tamar Campaign, centred in the Ujamaa Centre of the University of KwaZulu-Natal (see Tamar Campaign 2007).

22 I have not yet embarked on a volume on life stories of Ugandan LGBT refugees, which I will be co-writing with Adriaan van Klinken, as well as Raymond Brian and refugees from The Nature Network of Nairobi. In my capacity as co-editor of this Routledge Focus series I am also working towards commissioning volumes that will address marginalized perspectives. At the time of writing, a volume on rape culture and sex workers and another on male–male sexual abuse have been accepted and others, focusing on rape culture and persons in minority communities, including in the Two-Thirds World, have been commissioned.

23 For example, Gravett (2004: 279) and Penner and Cates (2007: 37.4).

24 There are also less widely used alternative meanings, such as colloquial ones, of 'rape'. Hence, in English idioms, 'I was raped' can mean 'I was ripped off' (see Hirsch 2018: 9). In teenage slang 'rape' can denote either low-level injury or damage (e.g. 'Wow, that maths test totally raped me')

or, alternatively, success (e.g. 'Oh yeah, I just raped that maths test') (cf. the use of 'kill' in similar expressions) (see Cohen 2012).

25 Hebrew uses a different alphabet. I am here transliterating Hebrew to give some approximation of what the Hebrew sounds like. This verb ('to take') is widely used in the Hebrew Bible for marriage (e.g. Gen 24:4, 7, 38, 40, 48). It can also denote physical force (e.g. Gen 14:12). For a fuller discussion see Gravett (2004: 282, n.10).

26 There is some dispute as to which of these three verbs best captures the act of rape. The Vulgate (early Latin version of the Bible) translates the first verb with *rapuit* (from *raptio*, see p. 2). Others suggest reading either two or all three words together as hendiadys to convey 'he raped'. For a summary see Van Wolde (2002a: 530).

27 Biblical Hebrew is an ancient Semitic language and the original language of the major part of the Hebrew Bible (or Old Testament). Smaller portions of the Hebrew Bible are written in a cognate Semitic language called Biblical Aramaic. The verbal system of Biblical Hebrew is founded on triliteral (three-letter) roots. Sometimes a root (including the root *'nh*) can appear in more than one verbal stem. Stem modifies meaning. Hence, a verb can appear in the *qal* stem (most often designating the simple active), or the *niphal* stem (most often designating the simple passive), or the *piel* stem (often designating an active intensive or a distinct meaning), among others. Understanding the denotation (let alone connotation) of Biblical Hebrew terms is difficult, because there are no longer any native speakers of Biblical Hebrew and no ancient lexica. Much about a word's or a text's meaning, or purpose, or original context, or development over time, or editing, can only be guessed at. One way to decode meaning is to examine the occurrences of a given word and to probe its contexts. Van Wolde (2002a: 530) examines *'nh* closely, explaining that verbs of this root occur 80 times in the Hebrew Bible. Fifty-seven are in the *piel* stem and 13 of these have a woman as a direct object. It is these occurrences that are of most relevance in terms of arguing for the translation of 'rape'.

28 The Douay-Rheims Bible has 'ravishing the virgin'. The verb 'ravish' is related to Latin *rapere* and can pertain to seizing and carrying away (someone) by force. The word is sometimes used with regard to rape – in the sense of forced sexual intercourse. More problematically, the word can also pertain to filling (someone) with delight, or rapture, which might be said to merge violent and romantic overtones in a disturbing way. The King James Version and the Jubilee Bible have 'defiled', and several other translations, similarly, '[he] humiliated' and '[he] humbled' (for a full list, see Bible Hub).

29 The shift from Dinah's brief agency as subject of an active verb (Genesis 34:1) to Dinah's status as grammatical object of a succession of verbs (Genesis 34:2) can also be taken to indicate violence and 'create contextual support for a reading of rape' (Gravett 2004: 283).

30 See below for a fuller discussion.

31 See Note 27.

32 Frymer-Kensky does consider 2 Samuel 13 to be a rape narrative. She also argues, however, like Van Wolde, that *'innâ* does not mean rape but 'to treat someone improperly in a way that degrades or disgraces them by

disregarding the proper treatment due people in each status' (Frymer-Kensky 1998: 87).

33 For a rebuttal see Graybill (Forthcoming).

34 Given Schulte's contrast with 'modern understanding', 'biblical rape' probably pertains to rape in 'biblical times' – a rather murky time-zone that covers easily a millennium.

35 Scholz (2005: 36.18 and n.34) and others recognize associations between the Christian Right and a pseudo-objectivist approach.

36 I have developed this point with reference to feminism elsewhere (Stiebert 2016: 117 and n.70). On Schulte as apologist for the biblical rape story of Bathsheba, see Chapter 1, Note 80 (p. 41).

37 It is not, however, the case that trauma is acknowledged equally for all, or that sympathy is extended equally to all victims of rape. There is a hierarchy of 'respectability' concerning rape victims, which determines how sympathy and outrage are accorded. It is well documented that young, white, middle-class, female victims of rape receive more media coverage and more public sympathy than poor black females (Gaertner *et al.* 1982; Sanyal 2019: 85–113). Sex workers who are raped receive very little coverage or sympathy and yet women in the sex work industry are documented as suffering acutely high rates of sexual assault and rape (Mulvihill 2018: 225). The situation is similar with refugees (Sanyal 2019: 94–95). Responses to rape are also affected by factors such as whether the rape victim was perceived as 'asking for it', indicated (with many female victims of rape) by what she was wearing, how much she may have had to drink and whether she was perceived as being promiscuous. See, for instance, Serisier (2017) and Phipps (2009), as well as Chapter 2, on rape myths and rape culture.

38 The imperative for language to convey experienced truth, including of awful, even unspeakable, experience, is central to June Jordan's writing. This applies to writing poignant and powerful poetry about her experience of rape and about the rape of others (see Kinloch 2006: 139–40).

39 Some biblical commentators state that marriage for females in ancient Israel took place imminently after puberty (e.g. Blenkinsopp 1997: 77) – for which I do not see any explicit or even particularly compelling evidence anywhere in the Bible. The Hebrew Bible has little to say about either marriage or consent, and nothing about an age of either consent or marriage-ability. I have argued elsewhere that there is also little evidence or mention of child marriage or sexual abuse of children, but that this cannot be taken to mean it did not happen (Stiebert 2016: 78).

40 Blyth (2010) challenges the erasure of rape accounts by focusing on the silence of Dinah in Genesis 34 and counterpointing this with contemporary accounts by rape survivors. Her subtle and poignant treatment of the biblical text, alongside directly expressed evidence of the brutality and harmfulness of rape, powerfully resists misnaming and suppressing rape and validates rape victims' experiences.

41 With regard to Hebrew, I have focused particularly on words of the root *'nh*. But other vocabulary, too, can be descriptive of rape. Hence the root *tpś*, sometimes denoting the act of seizing someone with the intent to have sex with them, is descriptive of rape or rape attempt in some biblical passages. Potiphar's wife tries to seize Joseph (Genesis 39:12) in an attempt to have sex with him against his will, for example. Another word that denotes

rape is from the root *šgl*. This appears to be an obscenity and is regularly substituted with the less profane *škv* (one of the verbs designating Shechem's action in Genesis 34:2, see p. 5 and Note 26). The verbal root *šgl* designates the rape of women as a form of punishment in both Deuteronomy (28:30) and the Prophets (punishment of Jerusalem in Zechariah 14:2 and of Babylon in Isaiah 13:16). For a fuller discussion see Gravett (2004: 289–90).

1 The Bible and #MeToo

#MeToo (or the Me Too movement)[1]

#MeToo is associated first and foremost with a social media driven digital feminist activist movement[2] that spread suddenly and remarkably quickly starting in late 2017. This movement sought, first, to expose the extent of sexual harassment, assault, and discrimination and, second, to rally solidarity and support for resisting these scourges. Its primary and distinctive tactic has been to trigger a deluge of revelations about sexual abuse, ranging from microaggressions to rape,[3] so that victims and survivors could find strength in numbers and collectively challenge perpetrators and rape-supportive social mechanisms.[4]

Both feminist activists and victims of sexual harassment and assault have been speaking loudly and publicly about the magnitude of the problem for years, even decades.[5] But none the less it remained 'obscured by both social stigma and the inadequacy of the criminal justice system' with only the occasional high-profile case (such as that of Roman Polanski or Dominique Strauss-Kahn) hitting the headlines (Popova 2019: 5). The movement's primary catalysts were the publication in the *New York Times* (Kantor and Twohey 2017) and *The New Yorker* (Farrow 2017) in October 2017 of articles reporting dozens of accusations by women of sexual misconduct, including rape, perpetrated by US mogul film producer Harvey Weinstein. The movement rapidly went viral, particularly when US actor Alyssa Milano used Twitter to rally victims of sexual harassment to add their voice declaring 'me too'. This grew rapidly into a swelling tide of resistance that demonstrated and testified to the magnitude of the problem. The problem itself – namely, widespread, even endemic and systemic, sexual harassment, abuse, and violence – was far from new. Accusations against Weinstein alone reached back three decades. Also, by 2017 a considerable number of other scandals had already hinted ominously at the range and depth and spread of sexual abuse. Be it in Catholic congregations across the globe, in Protestant churches, in Mormon and Mennonite and Hasidic communities,[6] in sports clubs, children's homes, exclusive boarding schools, in the military, on campuses and in hospitals, in institutions of government and in the commercial sector, sexual exploitation was in evidence and sometimes rife. Very many revelations disclosed abuses of power and exploitation of the vulnerable, who were, disproportionately, women and girls.[7]

The Me Too movement may have risen to wide public consciousness in 2017, but it had already been founded back in 2006 by African-American civil rights activist Tarana Burke.[8] Struck by her own inability to help a teenage girl who confided in her about sexual abuse, Burke initiated 'Me Too', the campaign motto of which is 'empowerment through empathy', with the purpose that the most vulnerable in her own community, namely, young girls of colour, would not be isolated or alone but could find support, community, and a means to empowerment and healing.

Burke has since expressed the view that #MeToo has become 'unrecognisable' to her (Wakefield 2018). Others, too, have made the case that Burke's movement was co-opted, often with little or no mention of its roots in Black activism. Zahara Hill, to give one example of many, was quick to point out, already on 18 October 2017, that 'Black women were left out of the dialogue that spurred the movement [and] … quickly isolated' (Hill 2017).[9] And yet, Hill continues, Black women 'weren't excluded for lack of relation to conversation around sexual assault and misogyny's impact', given that 'Black women regularly experience sexual assault as well and are often coerced into silence' (Hill 2017). Moreover, she points out, 'the outrage simply wasn't there for the Black women [such as Jemele Hill and Leslie Jones] who were put in vulnerable positions by rich white men' (Hill 2017) – whereas it was for the predominantly white Hollywood female actors prominent in the early stages of #MeToo.[10] Others have seen the response to the TV documentary series *Surviving R. Kelly*, wherein young Black women detail the abuse, paedophilia, and predatory behaviour of R&B singer Robert 'R' Kelly (which he denies) as the moment when the movement finally returned to Black girls – albeit rather late: the series, based on allegations dating back decades, only aired in January 2019 (Tillet and Tillet 2019).

Another notable precursor to #MeToo is #YesAllWomen. This campaign responded directly to the Isla Vista massacre on 23 May 2014. Elliott Rodger killed six people and injured 14 more before shooting himself. Prior to his murder spree, Rodger disseminated his 'manifesto' and disclosed via a video on YouTube that he was motivated by hatred both for the men whose sexual prowess he envied and for the women who had rejected him sexually.[11] The hashtag was partly created in response to #NotAllMen, which aimed to demonstrate that not all men are like Rodger, or even sexist. The response hashtag retaliates with the counter that while not all men may be sexist, all women are confronted with sexism, and it encouraged women to share examples or stories of misogyny and violence. Within four days #YesAllWomen had been tweeted 1.2 million times.

A second hashtag phenomenon of 2014 was #BeenRapedNeverReported. This hashtag began to trend shortly after the emergence of allegations of sexual violence by Canadian radio host Jian Ghomeshi. The hashtag was created by two journalists in response to suggestions that Ghomeshi's accusers were lying, because, if they were telling the truth, they would have reported his acts of violence more promptly. Countering the myths around how victims of sexual violence 'should' respond, the hashtag documents why victims often do *not* report sexual violence *at all* (or why, if they do, reports are frequently delayed). Over several weeks, the hashtag became an archive of in the range of eight million tweets.

In 2016[12] there followed #NotOK, initiated by author and social media personality Kelly Oxford in response to a recording in 2005 in which Donald Trump boasted of kissing, groping, and aggressively pursuing sex with women. The recording was leaked during Trump's presidential campaign[13] and the then nominee brushed it aside as 'locker room banter'. Oxford led the social media revolt to resist the notion that any such conduct is acceptable or excusable. Sharing her own story of first assault, being grabbed by the crotch as a 12-year-old while travelling on a city bus, Oxford asked others to join her. In the first 24 hours, 9.7 million women shared their stories.[14]

But 2017 marked a turning point. This was the year not only of feminist digital activism but of women's protests on the streets. The Women's March on 21 January 2017, the day following the inauguration of President Donald Trump, constituted the largest single-day protest in modern US history, with estimates ranging from 3.3 to 5.6 million marchers. Many more marched in solidarity in countries beyond the USA. And then, later that year, overtaking #YesAllWomen, 4.7 million people in 12 million posts on Facebook alone responded within 24 hours to Alyssa Milano's #MeToo rallying cry of 15 October. The movement gathered momentum extraordinarily quickly and led to the deposition of a number of public figures. Weinstein was promptly, roundly, and publicly condemned and has mostly withdrawn from the public domain, although he has mounted a legal challenge and is denying all allegations of non-consensual sexual contact. Others followed: among them, in the USA, the actor Kevin Spacey, television journalist Charlie Rose and news anchor Matt Lauer; and, in the UK, Defence Secretary Michael Fallon, to cite a few very prominent examples.[15]

Two years after its inception, the movement still continues to demonstrate efficacy, direct impact, and consequences – including well beyond the USA from which it first emanated. This is demonstrated, for example, by Minister M. J. Akbar's resignation from the Indian parliament (Suri 2018) and by Pakistani celebrity actor and musician Ali Zafar's emotional denial of harassment allegations (Hemery and Singh 2019) that followed a deluge of declarations of sexual impropriety in the wake of South Asia's #MeToo gaining momentum.[16] Other responses include the Japanese government's requirement for senior civil servants to undertake anti-sexual harassment training prior to being considered for promotion, Jamaica's new sexual harassment bill, a New Zealand doctors' union's launch of an investigation into sexual harassment in the medical profession, India's Telugu film industry's announcement of a sexual harassment redressal forum, and Australia's national inquiry on sexual harassment (see Sen 2018).

Milena Popova has called #MeToo 'the most visible expression … to date' of the endeavour to peel back the layers of rape culture and to dismantle the power structures in which it is enmeshed (Popova 2019: xii). Its resonance and success is perhaps indicated most memorably by the featuring of The Silence Breakers as *Time* magazine 'Person of the Year 2017'. The Silence Breakers is a diverse group of predominantly women which has spoken out against sexual exploitation; the group comprises not only celebrities (such as Ashley Judd and Taylor Swift), but also lobbyist Adama Iwu, software engineer Susan Fowler, activist Tarana Burke, and an anonymous hospital worker, among others. Another indication is the presence of #MeToo in advertising, notably in the Gillette campaign entitled 'We Believe: The Best Men Can Be', featuring news clips reporting on #MeToo alongside images showing sexism in films and elsewhere. The ad immediately went viral, with more than four million views on YouTube in 48 hours. Advertising is an industry that depends on instant recognition (in this case, recognition of #MeToo) and from an advertiser's perspective the campaign was stunningly successful.[17]

#MeToo has also spawned another movement called 'Time's Up', which acknowledges that class and colour in particular have considerable impact on vulnerability to sexual harassment and abuse. Founded by Hollywood celebrities on 1 January 2018, Time's Up raises money for its legal defence fund in order to provide for victims of sexual violence, particularly those who encounter it in the workplace. The fund is aimed at and being accessed by those most vulnerable to sexual assault who are least likely to be able to afford adequate legal representation, notably women on low incomes.

#MeToo has been criticised (like #YesAllWomen before it) for a number of reasons and from different angles. As well as Hill's (2017) critique, mentioned above, others have noted the movement's lack of inclusiveness and its propensity to give a greater platform to those who are more privileged than to those most vulnerable to sexual violence. Other criticisms focus on the conflation of microaggressions with violent physical assault, of succumbing to political correctness,[18] 'witch-hunting' of persons who have not committed any sexual offence[19] or 'only' an offence that is arguably insufficiently serious to merit public criticism, and on not doing enough to tackle sexual violence.

But by any measure, the scale and impact of the viral and global #MeToo campaign has been immense. While it is sometimes referred to as the 'MeToo *moment*', the movement's influence has been and continues to be sustained. Alongside its persistent presence in popular media, evidence for this also comes in the form of multiple book-length publications.[20] Again, like the movement itself, these publications, first, are often centred on feminism and, second, incorporate self-disclosure. They are not, however, of one voice. Two examples illustrating this are Roxane Gay's *Not That Bad: Dispatches from Rape Culture* (2018) and Germaine Greer's *On Rape* (2018).

Gay opens her book with an account of her rape and its grave consequences:

> When I was twelve years old, I was gang-raped in the woods behind my neighborhood by a group of boys with the dangerous intentions of bad men. It was a terrible, life-changing experience. Before that, I had been naive, sheltered. I believed people were inherently good and that the meek should inherit. I was faithful and believed in God. And then I didn't. I was broken. I was changed. I will never know who I would have been had I not become the girl in the woods.
>
> (Gay 2018: ix)

What follows is an anthology of accounts testifying over and over again to the long-term harm and damage caused not only by rape but also by sexual harassment and even microaggressions. The purpose is to harness

Gay's hope that due to #MeToo 'something in this deeply fractured culture is … changing' and to make a vocal contribution to the movement (Gay 2018: xii).

Rather differently, Germaine Greer, not long before the publication of her book, claimed in an interview at the 2018 Hay Festival that most rapes are 'lazy, careless and insensitive … bad sex' and 'don't involve any injury whatsoever'.[21] Greer also recalled her own physically violent experience of rape at the age of 18 and stated that women are not destroyed by rape but rather 'bloody annoyed' (Brown 2018). She characterized #MeToo as 'whingeing' (Flood 2018; Kaplan 2018).

Greer's book goes on in a similar vein to say that fear of rape is largely 'irrational', because '[a]n elbow, a thumb even, can do you more harm than a penis', hence, '[i]t is a nonsense for our daughters to be more frightened of penises than our sons are of knives or guns' (Greer 2018: 53). Greer's comments are very much at odds with the bulk of first-hand rape testimony, as well as with clinical research findings regarding rape victims, and are likely to be calculatedly provocative and polemical. She can indeed speak for herself – however unusual her rape response may be – because there is no single or uniform response to rape. Speaking for 'women' or 'raped persons' as a collective is, however, problematic and for all her assertions, I do not see how Greer can claim special authority.

These two publications attest to the poly-vocality of feminism[22] and to the impact of and strong responses to #MeToo. Nearly two years after its inception, #MeToo is still very much around and, as I will go on to discuss, its resonance and reach are extensive and can be brought also to a nuanced and critical reading of texts of sexual violence in the Bible.

Gender-based and sexual violence in the Bible[23]

Having demonstrated the influence of #MeToo and the spotlight it has cast on the extent of sexual violence in the present, let me turn next to the Bible. The Hebrew Bible is a text marked by violence of many kinds. And, as I argued in the Introduction, it includes depictions of and references to sexual threat, harassment, abuse, and assault. A comprehensive examination of violence vocabulary by David Clines makes this very clear. Adopting 'a largely physical definition of violence, … typically injury done especially to the body' (Clines 2018: 6–7), he establishes that there are around 500 Hebrew terms for violence and that 'occurrences of violence total some 10,033', or, put differently, 'on average, there are more than six instances of violence on every page of the Hebrew Bible' (Clines 2018: 3). Concerning language pertaining to sex, Clines writes,

> This may be a contentious issue, but I would argue that all the language about sex describes acts of violence to the body of another. I found no case where the language of sex referred to an act of mutual desire. In every case sex is the action of a male: a male 'knows *(yd')*', 'comes into *(bw' 'el)*' a woman (or another man); in the four cases where a woman is the grammatical subject of *yd'* used sexually, the verb is always negated (the woman 'had not known' a man). It is not relevant to ask whether in some examples there is consent, for ... an action may be violent even if the person acted upon has given consent. The terms 'to take *(lqch)* a woman' and 'to give *(ntn)* a woman' (still astonishingly used in our own culture) mean no more than the transfer of a woman from the authority of her father to that of her husband (with the additional imposition of sexual services). To call this 'marriage' can only be a euphemism. I do not deny that in ancient Israel there was mutual desire and mutual sexual activity. I am just registering the fact that there is no language expressing mutuality.
>
> (Clines 2018: 17–18)

Clines' points here will be important as I go on to examine texts of sexual harassment and violence in the Bible. These will not be confined only to depictions of bodily injury and physical violence, as in Clines' semantic analysis, but will also include verbal and implied threats.

There is no analysis comparable to Clines' concerning violence in the New Testament. The supersessionist notion, however, that the Old Testament (that is, the Hebrew Bible) is violent while the New Testament is somehow all about 'things being better now' can be roundly challenged. Shelly Matthews (2017: 33) explains this notion as a form of Christian Marcionism.[24] But in the New Testament, too, there is plenty of violence committed by both humans and God: 'this collection of scriptures is not innocent of the ideologies that both inspire ... violence and sanction that violence as God-ordained' (Matthews 2017: 34). First of all, crucifixion is a gruesome and exceedingly violent form of torture (Hengel 1977) and some scholars have proposed that even prior to being nailed to the cross Jesus was brutalized, including sexually humiliated, as is hinted at in repeated mention of his being stripped and exposed (Tombs 1999). Violence is also present elsewhere and extends from name-calling (Matthew 23:15; Titus 1:12), which includes examples of anti-Jewish rhetoric (John 8:44), to the casual mention of slavery[25] and threats of beating (Luke 12:45–47), inculcating women to be silent and submissive on account of primordial transgression (1 Timothy 2:11–14), gory punishment (2 Thessalonians 1:6–9) and vitriol about immorality deserving death (Romans 1:32), to the gruesome images of battles, plagues, and bloodshed in Revelation (e.g. Revelation 19:17–21).[26] Sexualized violence also receives mention in Revelation, and will be discussed below.

Some commentators of the New Testament, notably Elisabeth Schüssler Fiorenza, also point out that the

> Christian proclamation of the kyriarchal politics of submission and its attendant virtues of self-sacrifice, docility, subservience, obedience, suffering, unconditional forgiveness, male authority and unquestioning surrender to G*d's will [e.g. 1 Peter 2:18–3:1; 2 Timothy 2:8–12] *covertly* advocate in the name of G*d patriarchal practices of victimization.
>
> (Schüssler Fiorenza 2011: 110)[27]

Like Phyllis Trible in the area of feminist Hebrew Bible studies (see below), Schüssler Fiorenza has had enormous and comparable impact in the area of the study of women, including of violence against women, but in New Testament studies.[28]

Matthews (2017) uses Schüssler Fiorenza's ideas to make a case for the violence of 1 Corinthians 11:2–16, arguing that there is violence both *in the text* and in the outworkings *of the text* in Christian communities. Matthews points out that the passage from 1 Corinthians fulfils an important part in 'the household codes that directly exhort the submission of wives, slaves, and children to their husband, master, or father (Eph[esians] 5:21–6:9; Col[ossians] 3:18–4:1; 1 Pet[er] 2:18–3:7)' (Matthews 2017: 35).[29] She is aware of alternative ways of reading verse 3 – of the man (or husband) being the head of his woman (or wife) – but notes that the dominant interpretation pertains to the establishment of a hierarchy privileging males over females. Matthews also notes that the odd inculcation that a woman ought to cover her head 'because of the angels' (1 Corinthians 11:10) has been read in terms of a threat of sexual violence. Just as the sons of God saw beautiful women and raped them (Genesis 6:2–4), so, because a woman's hair is enticing or because 'a woman's head functions metonymically as her genitals … the argument proceeds, [that] through uncovering their heads and exposing their sexuality, … women are making themselves vulnerable to rape by the angels … who harbor uncontrollable lust' (Matthews 2017: 39).[30] Matthews is careful to point out that texts such as 1 Corinthians 11 'are not overtly advocating sexual abuse, rape, or femicide' but also, that 'such subordinationist rhetoric is still violent rhetoric, inscribing women as a diminished form of humanity, second to man and farther from God than man in the established hierarchy' and that such 'diminishment paves the way for more extreme acts of exploitation and victimization' (Matthews 2017: 38).

Notwithstanding evidence of gender fluidity and gender ambiguity in the Bible,[31] sexual violence is most often cast in binary (that is, male-on-female) terms and is thereby gendered. Assumptions incline towards heteronormativity – that is, the notion that males are, hierarchically, above females; males are heterosexual (that is, attracted to and sexually active with females); and males take sexual initiative. Moreover, this is depicted as 'natural' or 'normative'.[32]

Sexual violence in the Bible is not only gendered but also spectral, ranging from hints and implications, lewd comment (Judges 5:30),[33] threats of male rape (e.g. Genesis 19:5) and implied permission to rape girl children (Numbers 31:18) or one's daughter (Genesis 19:8), to depictions of rape, including incestuous rape (2 Samuel 13), gang rape (Judges 19:25), and mass abduction for the purpose of rape 'marriage' (Judges 21:21).[34]

Before focusing on the dominant manifestation of male-on-female sexual violence in the Bible, it is important to mention that there are exceptions. The Bible, after all, is a diverse concatenation of texts, composed, edited, and collected together over centuries. It is a product of many times and contexts; its authors are unknown and the selection criteria for inclusion of texts in what is now called 'the Bible' can only be guessed at. It is not surprising, consequently, that what the Bible contains is internally diverse and variegated and sometimes contradictory. There are patterns and also departures from patterns. So, while the bulk of depictions show sexual violence perpetrated by men against women, which will go on to become the primary focus of this volume,[35] other gendered dynamics exist.

There are quite a number of indications of male–male sexual violence. I am using the designation male–male rape (or abuse or sexual violence), not 'homosexual rape' *(pace* Stone 1996: 79) because the distinction is important. In contemporary language usage 'homosexuality' is understood as a sexual orientation – that is, the tendency of a male or female to be sexually attracted to and fulfilled by a member of the same rather than a different sex (i.e. heterosexuality), or to both males and females (bisexuality). Sexual acts with a member of the same sex can result from homosexual attraction – but are not constitutive of homosexual orientation. Naming male–male rape 'homosexual', however, suggests that rape *is* a matter of attraction. But instead, rape is above all a matter of power and humiliation – not sexual desire.[36]

Male–male rape is threatened in two places in the Hebrew Bible: by the men of Sodom (Genesis 19:5)[37] and by the men of Gibeah (Judges 19:22). In both cases, a counter offer is made by a host protecting the male visitor/s being threatened. In Sodom, Lot offers his two virgin daughters (Genesis 19:8) and the old man at Gibeah offers the visiting Levite's wife and his own virgin daughter (Judges 19:24). Such offers would make no sense if the thugs of Sodom or Gibeah were indeed homosexual. More likely is that these men's intention is to humiliate another man by raping him. As Ken Stone explains, such an act may have been understood, heteronormatively, as feminizing a man (i.e. by placing him in a role where he is sexually penetrated, a position 'properly' associated with females) and thereby moving him socially downward (Stone 1996: 79).

The case has been made that the odd story fragment of Genesis 9:18–29 also conceals or hints at male–male sexual abusiveness. Here, when Noah awakes from a drunken sleep, he knows 'what his younger son [Ham] had done to him' (Genesis 9:24) and the expression that Ham sees 'the nakedness of his father' (Genesis 9:22) hints darkly at incest.[38] It has been proposed that Ham has raped Noah.[39] If so, this could again best be understood as an attempt to gain or to assert dominance – in this case by sexually humiliating a social superior: Noah, Ham's father.[40]

Concerning male–male sexual abuse in the New Testament,[41] Christopher Zeichmann (2018) discusses the story of the centurion and his servant (Matthew 8:5–13; Luke 7:1–10). This story has been explored by a number of biblical scholars in terms of its homoerotic potentialities. This is based first, on what is known of Roman pederasty and second, on the possible meaning of certain key terms in Koine, the Greek of the New Testament. In the Roman context, pederasty, or the sexual pursuit of male youths by older Roman men, appears to have been permissible. Just as in classical Greece, however, pederasty was circumscribed by laws and conventions.[42] In Rome, penetration of freeborn youths was illegal. The only boys a man could sexually penetrate legally were either slaves or his own former slaves, known as 'freedmen'. Slaves had no protection under the law against rape.[43] The vocabulary of the similar stories in Matthew and Luke, meanwhile, makes clear that the relationship is between a freeborn and dominant person (the centurion) and a person who is subordinate and a slave *(doulos,* Luke 7:2, 4, 10).[44] The centurion also calls his slave *pais* (another word for 'servant', Matthew 8:6, 8; Luke 7:7) and describes him as *entimos* ('dear', Luke 7:2) both of which have been said to hint at pederastic attraction.[45] For Zeichmann, eroticizing, let alone romanticizing, the relationship is, however, profoundly problematic given that the slave cannot exercise free will and is, consequently, unlikely to be a consenting participant in any (hypothetical) sexual activity.[46]

Alongside mention and intimation of male–male sexual violence there is also reference in the Bible of female–male sexual harassment – notably, the story of Potiphar's wife (Genesis 39).[47] In this story Joseph is a servant, or slave (Hebrew *'eved*), in the household of his Egyptian master Potiphar, a high-ranking official. Potiphar's wife becomes attracted to Joseph (Genesis 39:7) and, after he refuses her demand for sex, harasses him day after day (Genesis 39:10). Eventually, she propositions him again and – after Joseph escapes – accuses him, wrongfully, of attempted rape (Genesis 39:12–18).[48]

Another text to mention is the disturbing story of Lot's daughters (Genesis 19:30–38).[49] According to a face-value reading of the text, on consecutive nights the two daughters each get their father Lot so drunk that he, without knowing or remembering what he is doing, impregnates them. Given that the daughters connive to have sex with someone who is unable to give consent, this is an instance of female–male rape.[50]

Female–female interactions receive considerably less attention in the Bible than male–male or male–female interactions.[51] Any suggestion of sexualized violence between females is also rare. An example might be the harsh treatment Sarai inflicts on her slave Hagar. After Sarai has handed Hagar to Abram,[52] because she wants Hagar to bear a child on her behalf (Genesis 16:2), she becomes angry with Hagar who, following conception, despises Sarai (Genesis 16:4).[53] In this context of interpersonal tension between women and in a text overshadowed by rape (because Hagar's consent is implausible and certainly unmentioned), Sarai is said to have 'dealt harshly with [Hagar]' (New Revised Standard Version [NRSV] – using the verb of the root *'nh*, which, as discussed, can have sexually aggressive, including rape-denotative meanings.

Thus, male-on-male and female-on-male sexual harassment, abuse, or violence are there in the Bible. Female-on-female sexualized violence is harder to identify. By far the most occurrent is male-on-female sexual violence. The Bible, in particular the Hebrew Bible, is punctuated with male-on-female violence and rape – which is why I will go on to argue (see Chapter 2) that the Bible reflects a rape culture.

Even if one does not accept Clines' assertion, cited above, that 'all the language about sex [in the Bible] describes acts of violence to the body of another' (Clines 2018: 17), there is plenty to point to that is either suggestive, or unambiguously descriptive, of forced penetrative sex of an unwilling victim. In other words, there is a lot about rape in the Bible. What follows is not exhaustive but should make this claim indisputable.

Genesis 34 is among the biblical passages most often identified as a rape text. This is the story, already alluded to above (p. 5), where Shechem, a Hivite prince, rapes Dinah, the daughter of Jacob and Leah.[54] The narrative begins with Dinah going out 'to see the daughters of the land' (Genesis 34:1). Todd Penner and Lilian Cates refer to this as a 'momentary glimpse of agency' before Dinah comes to exist only in terms of 'the male gaze' (Penner and Cates 2007: 37.4). Both the fact that Dinah is identified first as the daughter of Leah, rather than Jacob, and that she actively goes out to visit non-Hebrew women,[55] has made her suspect since antiquity. Leah, the rabbis recalled, also exercised sexual forwardness: in exchange for some mandrakes collected by her eldest son, she received conjugal rights to her husband from Rachel, her sister and Jacob's favoured co-wife. Going to meet Jacob, Leah tells him that she has hired him (for sex) (Genesis 30:16). Is Dinah, like her mother, sexually forward, even sexually wayward? This was the question.[56] In the second verse, however, Shechem sees Dinah, takes her, has sex with her: he rapes her (Genesis 34:2). The first of the three verbs that convey Shechem's actions ('to take') refers to moving Dinah from one place to another; the second is a standard word for sexual intercourse; the third is from *'nh* and both qualifies and clarifies the preceding verb. This is the verb already mentioned, which frequently designates rape and the humiliation effected by rape.

Some commentators have challenged the view that Genesis 34:2 describes a rape. Both Lyn Bechtel (1994) and Ellen Van Wolde (2002a, 2002b), for example, argue that on the basis of Genesis 34 the conclusion that Shechem rapes Dinah cannot be substantiated. As already discussed, Van Wolde (2002a) argues that *'nh* nowhere pertains to a sexual act but to being denigrated and, moreover, that Dinah's consent receives no mention and probably does not matter. While, for Van Wolde (2002b), consent can neither be assumed nor denied, Dinah is, however, deemed to be defiled on account of sex with a foreign man. Bechtel (1994), too, maintains that none of the three verbs describing the sex act in Genesis 34:2 unequivocally means 'rape' and that *'nh* pertains to the lowering of Dinah's status, not to the forced nature of the sex act. She also contends that Shechem's 'love' (Hebrew *'hv*) for Dinah and his speaking to her heart (Genesis 34:3) and determining to marry her are atypical of a rapist's response following rape.[57]

I align myself with the many modern English translations (see p. 5) and with the majority of commentators[58] who point out that the most straightforward reading here is one of rape.[59] Here a man with high social standing and, quite possibly, a considerable sense of entitlement (cf. Genesis 34:4), simply takes the woman he wants – because he can. Dinah's voice and perspective do not receive mention. In all likelihood, her consent was irrelevant to her rapist. Consent, however, is unlikely and force and sexual penetration are indicated with little scope for ambiguity (Genesis 34:2). This is a rape text.

In addition to Genesis 34, three of the four focus texts in Phyllis Trible's (1984) seminal *Texts of Terror*[60] are rape texts. Two of these, Judges 19 and 2 Samuel 13, are possibly the most 'obvious' rape texts in the Bible. Both purport to depict events in Israel's history. Judges 19, aptly described by J. Cheryl Exum (2015 [1993]: 136) as among the 'most gruesome and violent [narratives] in the Bible', is set in pre-monarchial Israel (Judges 19:1) and tells the story of an unnamed Levite and his also unnamed wife. In the story the wife 'plays the harlot'[61] or becomes angry[62] (Judges 19:2), leaves her husband and returns to her father's house. After some months the Levite goes after her and eventually proceeds to return with her to his home in Ephraim. On the way, seeking to avoid lodgings among foreigners, the Levite accepts an invitation to stay overnight in the home of an old Ephraimite man in Gibeah. During the night, the old man's house is surrounded by thugs[63] (Judges 19:22) who demand 'to know' the visitor. The old man attempts to negotiate with the thugs, which involves the offer of his own virgin daughter and the visitor's wife as rape substitutes.[64] He tells the men to rape (*'nh*) *them* instead and to do with *them* whatever is 'good in their eyes' but not to commit an outrage against the man (Judges 19:24).[65] The men do not relent, at which point the Levite brings out to them his wife and they rape and abuse her all night (Judges 19:25).[66] Violence and a sense of menace are all too clear: the men are designated thugs and the verbs indicate sex and brutality. This is rape. Brutal gang rape. Brutality leads to the wife's death. The detail of her falling at the door, her hands on the threshold, is affecting (Judges 19:27). For a character who had no voice in a story in which she played a significant part, this dying gesture is acutely articulate, performative of unspeakable atrocity and injustice.[67]

The second text of terror is the account of the rape of David's only named daughter, Tamar (2 Samuel 13). This rape text in the Bible is unusual in that the narrator makes an attempt to depict the damaging and devastating effect of rape on the victim.[68] Elsewhere no attempt is made to capture the rape victim's perspective. In this story, Tamar's brother Amnon, the royal firstborn, becomes obsessed with his sister. He desires her but is aware he should not act on his desire because

Tamar is a virgin (2 Samuel 13:2). After being advised by a crafty relative, Amnon contrives a situation where he and Tamar are alone. He orders her to 'lie with' him (2 Samuel 13:11). Tamar refuses, urging him not to force her (the word is from *'nh* and, again, clearly pertains to force and denigration – that is, to rape)[69] and not to commit a terrible deed (the Hebrew word is *nebalâ*; cf. Genesis 34:7, also in reference to rape). In this story, more clearly than in any other in the Bible, unwillingness and absence of consent are explicit. Tamar reiterates her refusal, telling Amnon that rape would lead to shame for her and make him unworthy. Appealing to the only person of higher status and authority, she urges Amnon to speak to the king – presumably to arrange a formal union (2 Samuel 13:13). But, being stronger than Tamar, Amnon rapes her (2 Samuel 13:14).[70] Not only is this story unusual in that absence of consent is made clear, but also in describing the aftermath of the rape. Amnon's reaction after the rape is one of abhorrence and rejection towards Tamar (2 Samuel 13:15). Tamar identifies what was done to her as an evil (2 Samuel 13:16). After she is evicted, she tears her robe (which had signified her status as a virgin royal daughter) and performs other mourning actions. Like the Levite's wife's gesture of reaching wordlessly for the threshold, Tamar performs the great wrong that was done to her.[71] She does not speak again but remains desolate (2 Samuel 13:20).[72] As in Judges, following the rape of a woman, revenge is brutal and enacted by men.

The third rape text in *Texts of Terror* is the story of Hagar and Sarai. In the earlier part of this story, Sarai, the primary wife of Abram, is unable to conceive. She determines to use Hagar, her slave, as her surrogate and gives her to Abram to bear a child that will subsequently be hers (Genesis 16:1–4).[73] While I classify Genesis 16 as a rape story – given that Hagar's consent to being handed to Abram for sex and surrogacy is neither recorded nor likely – Trible's (1984) emphasis in her chapter is not on rape but on how this text demonstrates Sarai's brutal treatment of Hagar.[74] Trible's choice not to highlight Hagar's status as rape victim and sex slave is striking. Perhaps it constitutes a failure to recognize Hagar as such. Both rape of slaves and rape in warfare are not always or even often foregrounded and named as rape in the Bible.

As with the centurion's slave, discussed above, there is no mention in the biblical text of enslaved women having any significant legal protection, nor is there indication of any attempt to seek their consent to sex. Hagar is simply handed to Abram by Sarai and, in similar fashion, Rachel hands over Bilhah to Jacob (Genesis 30:3–7) and Leah hands over Zilpah, also to Jacob (Genesis 30:9–12). Reuben also lies with Bilhah – which is depicted as an affront to Jacob, not Bilhah (Genesis 35:22; 49:3–4).

The law of Leviticus also suggests slave women's susceptibility to rape and that such rape was accorded comparatively little seriousness. Here, it says that if a man has sex with a slave woman who has been designated for another man but has not been redeemed or granted her freedom, then the death penalty does not apply. Instead, the man must provide a guilt offering, upon which he is forgiven (Leviticus 19:20–22). This is not considered a case either of adultery (cf. Deuteronomy 22:22–24) or rape of a betrothed woman (cf. Deuteronomy 22:25), in both of which cases the death penalty applies. The likeliest reason is that even less than with 'freed' women, slave women had no legal protection and no ability to consent. They are depicted as rapable.[75] Then again, being a sole or primary wife, as opposed to a secondary wife or a slave, does not seem to make women entirely 'freed' given that Abram still puts Sarai at risk of sexual exploitation to protect himself from more powerful men – Pharaoh (Genesis 12)[76] and Abimelech (Genesis 20).[77]

Legal texts, moreover, permit that a captive woman, the spoils of war, can be handed over, following a preparatory ritual, for sex – that is, rape (Deuteronomy 21:11–14).[78] Deuteronomy 21 does say that if the man who 'takes' (v.11) the captive woman no longer wants her, he must not sell her – presumably, into slavery. The reason given for this is that the man has committed *'nh* against her (v.14). This verb, as already mentioned, can mean '(he) humiliated, or dishonoured, or humbled (her)', but it can also mean, '(he) raped (her)'. The law permits use of the captive woman for sex but the rape and degradation committed against her are also acknowledged – albeit, not to the extent that the man's actions are prohibited.

There is plenty in the Bible to suggest that rape was part of war (as it remains to this day) (e.g. Lamentations 5:11; Zechariah 14:2; cf. Judges 16:4; see Thistlewaite 1993; Washington 1998). Women raped in war are depicted, essentially, as collateral damage and war spoils in conflicts between warring groups (see Keefe 1993). Revenge for Dinah's rape, too, transpires in seizing Hivite women and girls as part of the booty (Genesis 34:29), maybe for the purpose of revenge rape. Elsewhere, female captives in war were used for sex – that is, raped (e.g. Judges 21:11–14) – and were possibly sometimes very young (Numbers 31:17–18). While descriptions of rape in war are sometimes a device to arouse pathos (Lamentations 1:8–10),[79] rape is also 'part of the furniture' of war, and mentioned in passing in song to account for the delay of victorious armies (Judges 5:30). Rape in war is also depicted as permissible, advantageous, and as divinely mandated.

Rape in the Bible is often an expression of power – and not only of victorious armies, as in the examples above, but also of sons of God

(Genesis 6:2) and high-status men. As with Shechem and Dinah, when King David 'takes' and 'lies with' Bathsheba (2 Samuel 11:4), Bathsheba's consent is unstated.[80] David, as the story unfolds, is rebuked by Nathan, his prophet, for adultery and for engineering the murder of Bathsheba's husband (2 Samuel 12:9), but he is not rebuked for the rape he has committed. David's taking of Bathsheba expresses and asserts his power.[81] Just as David's son Amnon used his power to take and rape Tamar, the woman he desired, so David and other powerful men rape: it is an act which expresses and performs masculine power. Hence, when Absalom, another of David's sons, stages an uprising against his father, the king, he, apparently strategically, following the advice of a highly regarded counsellor (2 Samuel 16:23), publicly rapes David's wives who had been left behind when the king escaped his son's onslaught (2 Samuel 16:22). Absalom's rape of his father's wives is intended to perform and display his assertion of superior power.[82]

Rape in the Bible is almost[83] always understood as occurring outside of marriage[84] – though rape can be a catalyst for marriage (Genesis 34:2–4; Judges 21:23), or marriage a 'solution' to 'make the best of' rape (Deuteronomy 22:29; 2 Samuel 13:13, 16). Rape is portrayed as polluting, denigrating, and humbling. Even if a woman was virtuous and resisted rape, like Tamar, and even if generous amends and marriage are offered following a rape, as in the case of Dinah, rape is defiling. Lack of fault or attempts at restitution do not alter this. Rape renders Tamar desolate (2 Samuel 13:20) and Dinah defiled (Genesis 34:13, 27).[85] While other types of sex – such as adulterous sex (cf. Leviticus 18:20) – are also depicted as shocking and defiling, the association between rape and profound humiliation for the rape victim is very pronounced.

Because rape is clearly so damaging to the victim, rape is present also in descriptions of punishment – particularly in the writings of the Prophets. The punishment of Babylon, personified in the book of Isaiah as a woman ('virgin daughter of Babylon', Isaiah 47:1), is humiliation on account of her lack of mercy, her arrogance and wickedness (Isaiah 47:6–7, 10). The sexual overtones of this punishment are clear. Hence, there is a reference to Babylon 'grinding', alongside images of 'her' being stripped, uncovered, and shamed (Isaiah 47:2–3). All of these are suggestive of rape.[86] In Jeremiah, very similar imagery – the lifting up of skirts, suffering of violence, and shame (Jeremiah 13:22, 26) – are descriptive of punishment for abominations, adulteries, bestial neighing, and lewd harlotries (Jeremiah 13:27). Robert Carroll (2006 [1986]: 304) interprets the image as a referred metaphor, reflecting actual wartime practice, and draws attention to the full force of the brutality of this 'poetic justice for sins committed':

Jerusalem has become a violated woman, a typical victim of invading warriors. The images used are graphic and violent. They are metaphors of the city's humiliation and defeat, but they are drawn from the real world of horrendous aggression directed against women in time of war and invasion. In such brutal times the women are led off to the invaders [Jeremiah] (38:23), stripped naked and savagely raped – their genitals suffer violence and their shameful humiliation is made a public spectacle. Metaphors and reality combine to portray a sickening picture of battered sexuality and torn flesh, an image of a culture invaded, raped and devastated.

(Carroll 2006 [1986]: 304)

Similarly, Israel's disobedience is likened to the unfaithfulness of the prophet Hosea's wife, Gomer. The punishment advocated here too – to strip and expose and to make 'her' (i.e. Gomer/Israel) a dried up wasteland (Hosea 2:3 [Hebrew 2:5]) – again recalls rape.[87] While the word is not the same as that denoting Tamar's desolation after her rape, the idea conveyed here, that rape is followed by a state of emptiness and destruction, is very similar. Most extensive, violent, and abhorrent is the woman metaphor of Ezekiel (Chs 16 and 23), which is cited as a quintessential example of the 'pornoprophetic'.[88] Here, after a catalogue of transgressions,[89] the punishment inflicted on Jerusalem is to strip her before a mob of her lovers (Ezekiel 16:37; 23:22) who will leave her naked and bare, stone her, stab her and burn her possessions (Ezekiel 16:39–41), fight her with an army, remove her nose and ears – and strip her and leave her exposed (Ezekiel 23:24–29). The rape imagery is particularly vicious and the metaphor acutely disturbing – all the more because it is God who legitimates and metes out the punishment.[90]

Similar images of rape as punishment occur also in the New Testament. The book of Revelation mentions a false prophetess, 'that woman Jezebel' (alluding to the proverbially abhorrent Phoenician queen of Israel, consort of King Ahab),[91] who will be 'cast into a bed ... of tribulation', which has ominous overtones of sexual violence (Revelation 2:22). As with the Ezekiel example above, the prophecy is identified as divine pronouncement ('the Revelation of Jesus Christ, which God gave Him ...', Revelation 1:1), which again makes the sexualized violence particularly disturbing due to its being divinely legitimated and initiated. Revelation also contains an example of a prophetic woman metaphor, reminiscent of the examples from Isaiah, Hosea, and Ezekiel, with a sinful city in need of punishment again depicted as a woman on whom sexualized violence is poured out. Hence, in Revelation 17 a woman called a harlot, or whore, will be made 'desolate and naked'.

Moreover, her flesh will be eaten and burned with fire (Revelation 17:15–18). Again, God is executor of this sexualized violence.[92]

Nevertheless, despite numerous texts depicting episodes of sexual violence that go unpunished (or that are even divinely mandated), there are biblical laws inculcating punishment for rape. These laws stress, above all, the importance of betrothal, which signifies to whom a woman belongs. An unbetrothed woman is the property of her father; a betrothed woman is the property of the man to whom she is betrothed. If a man has sex with a woman betrothed to another man both are to be killed – no room is made for the possibility that the woman may have been raped (Deuteronomy 22:22).[93] An elaboration specifies that if a man has sex with a betrothed virgin in a town, both are to be killed: the man, because he raped (from *'nh*) the virgin woman, and the woman 'because she did not cry out' (Deuteronomy 22:24). While there could be all sorts of reasons why a woman might not scream, her complicity in rape appears to be assumed if she does not cry out in a place where she might be heard. If a man overpowers a betrothed virgin in the open country, however, then only the man is to be executed, not the woman, who may have cried out but not been heard (Deuteronomy 22:25–27). If a virgin woman is not betrothed and a man seizes her and lies with her and they are found out, then the law specifies that the man pays the woman's father a sum of money (presumably as compensation for her lowered economic value; cf. Exodus 22:16–17). Only now is it elaborated upon that this is because the man has raped the woman (from the verb *'nh*). Moreover, in such cases the man and woman must marry with no possibility of divorce (Deuteronomy 22:28–29). In one sense, this is something of an invitation to marriage by rape (cf. Judges 21:20–23).[94] In these laws, women are depicted as the property of men; their virginity is a valuable asset; consent is assumed if a woman does not scream and marriage to a rapist is regarded as a 'solution' to 'the problem' of a defiled and devalued woman. The laws paint a bleak picture.

As demonstrated, there is a lot of sexual violence in the Bible and the majority of depictions describe male perpetrators and female victims. Depressingly, even biblical books widely praised for affirming women, namely, Song of Songs and the two books named after women, Ruth and Esther, are overshadowed by more sinister indications of sexual violence. Song of Songs has a prominent speaker who is presumed to be female. She yearns for her male lover (who describes her body and erotic appeal at length). She is the little sister of her protective brothers who seek to restrain her – by force if need be (Song 5:9) – and there are watchmen who beat her and take away her veil when they find her in the city streets in search of her beloved (Song 5:7).[95]

The book of Ruth, is often characterized as a pastoral idyll and a women's book but it, too, makes reference – rather casually – to the dangers of working alongside men in the fields. Boaz, a wealthy land-owner, instructs Ruth to stay near the women while working in his fields – something Ruth's mother-in-law Naomi impresses on Ruth, too (Ruth 2:22). Boaz also assures her that he has instructed the men not to touch her (Ruth 2:8–9).[96] This suggests dangerous working conditions – certainly for women. While Boaz seems to acknowledge the existence of menace and harassment, he later praises Ruth for not going after the men (Ruth 3:10) – as if, had she been molested, it might have been her fault after all.

Finally, although much is made of the book of Esther's comic elements and of it being a book celebrating a clever and beautiful Jewish queen, Esther also speaks of women who are groomed and marketed for sex. Hence, the text refers to beautiful young virgins brought to Ahasuerus of Persia from all over his kingdom (Esther 2:3). Each girl, following a regimen of beautification, is brought to the king for one night to delight him (Esther 2:12–17), which is strongly reminiscent of trafficking and sex work (see Dunbar 2018).

All of this demonstrates that sexualized and gendered violence is widely in evidence in much of the Bible. Neither texts that apparently foreground and celebrate women (such as the books of Ruth and Esther) nor the New Testament (sometimes characterized as being a tonic to the violence of the Hebrew Bible) are exempt from this generalization. #MeToo confirms the ubiquity of sexual violence right up to the present. In both the revelations of this movement and in biblical texts such violence is perpetrated most commonly by men against women and girls, although other gendered dynamics are also represented by both. Next, we will bring the two together and examine them in the light of rape myths and rape culture.

Notes

1 Technically, '#MeToo' is the hashtag, or metadata tag, used on the social network service Twitter as the mechanism for finding messages relating specifically to the Me Too movement – individuals publicly disclosing sexual harassment and abuse with a view to inciting solidarity, empowerment, and resistance. The hashtag has, however, become a shorthand designation for the movement itself and this is how '#MeToo' is widely used in this book.

2 The topic of 'popular misogyny' in twenty-first century media culture (e.g. endemic sexist trolling and the manosphere) is regarded by some as the male counterpart and by others as the opposition to digital feminism. A discussion of this important topic is beyond the scope of this volume; see Sarah Banet-Weiser (2015) for a brief summary. The important research of

Kathryn Barber (2018) focuses especially on religious ideologies and gender-based violence of the manosphere.

3 Sexual abuse is widely recognized as spectral. It ranges from microaggressions – that is, brief and often non-remarkable, day-to-day indignities of a verbal or behavioural (such as gestural) nature, which communicate hostile, discriminatory, or degrading slights and derogatory attitudes or implicit bias – to physical violence and torture aimed at either individuals, groups, or whole masses of people. Sexual abuse is not confined to physical violence (typically understood as injury done to the body) but extends to threats and humiliations and causes psychological and emotional damage and deprivation. Rape, meanwhile, is variously defined in different jurisdictions (see p. 2).

4 Rape-supportive manifestations point to rape culture (see Chapter 2).

5 Alongside Brownmiller and other second-wave feminists, prominent here are, in the US context, conversations and cases centred on Title IX and its stipulation that sexual harassment and assault constitute a form of discrimination on the basis of sex. Many of these focused on campus settings (see Minister 2018; Scholz 2018). On rape on US campuses see also the film *The Hunting Ground*.

6 See Filipovic (2013). There are numerous large-scale and brutal examples from non-European and non-North American contexts, such as the mass abductions and sexual enslavement by Boko Haram in Nigeria and the atrocities and sex slavery inflicted on Yazidi women by ISIS (the Islamic State of Iraq and Syria, also known by the names ISIL and Daesh). While the scourge of sexual and gender-based violence is global and #MeToo has had resonance worldwide, with India's Bollywood, for instance, reporting widespread abuse and harassment (see Suri 2018), my focus will be principally on one main hub of its influence, which lies in the Christian-dominant and Anglophone democracies of North America and Europe, as well as Australia and New Zealand.

7 For a range of examples, most from Anglophone democracies, including accusations of sexual assault by US President Donald Trump, the Australian Royal Commission into Institutional Responses to Child Sexual Abuse (2012–17), and the New Zealand 'Roast Busters' scandal, see Peters and Besley (2019: 459–462).

8 There have been other mass feminist movements aimed at publicizing and resisting violence against women. One notable example is the movement founded by Eve Ensler and her play *The Vagina Monologues*, written and first performed in 1996. The play has been translated into dozens of languages and performed all over the world. In 1998 Ensler launched V-Day, a global activist movement raising consciousness and funds through productions of the play in order to stop violence against women and girls.

9 See also Phipps (forthcoming): '#MeToo could largely be interpreted as a conversation between white people.'

10 For an excellent examination of #MeToo and the backlash against the movement, with particular focus on the notions of victim feminism and white woundedness, see Phipps (forthcoming).

11 Rodger has since become an 'incel' (involuntarily celibate) hero, see BBC News (2018).

12 Reports of mass sexual harassment on New Year's Eve 2015–16 in Cologne were another significant factor in propelling public outrage and mobilizing

change in the form of adapting Germany's legal definition of rape to a consent-centric one. As has been pointed out, the same event appears reliably to have been exploited also to fan simmering Islamophobic and anti-migrant attitudes (Popova 2019: 175; Sanyal 2019: 90–95).

13 See Chapter 2 and Chapter 2, Note 66.

14 I have mentioned only the best-known antecedents of #MeToo. There are very many more and diverse examples of digital feminist activism. Alongside the numerous individuals posting regularly on Twitter, Instagram, Facebook and in blogs on the topic of sexual violence, these include the website 'Hollaback!', which shares stories of street harassment alongside maps of locations using GPS technology, and 'Everyday Sexism', which was founded by Laura Bates and collects public posts of personal accounts of sexism, as well as the Tumblr site 'Who Needs Feminism?', which collates pictures of handcrafted signs explaining the importance of feminism. For a fuller discussion of these and other examples, as well as of the centrality of personal testimonials in feminist activism, see Mendes *et al.* (2019).

15 The number of high-profile men coerced or forced to resign following Weinstein's fall stood at 42 by mid-December 2017. More followed. Decades of accusations of sexual violence made by more than 60 women against actor Bill Cosby transpired in a conviction for three counts of aggravated indecent assault in September 2018. By far the most disclosures of #MeToo concern sexual assaults on younger women by heterosexual men (Peters and Besley 2019) but there are some exceptions. Kevin Spacey stands accused of sexual predation on males, including a male minor. There have also been allegations of women molesting male minors (e.g. the accusation that actor Asia Argento assaulted former co-star Jimmy Bennett when he was 17).

16 There are hashtags centred outside of the Anglophone world, such as #YoTambien (Spain and Latin America), #RiceBunny (China), and #Balancetonporc (France), as well as reports of the growing momentum of #MeToo in Egypt (Afify 2019), and Thailand (Ellis-Petersen 2019). Meanwhile, in New York, #MeToo was cited as one reason rape reports increased by 22 per cent in 2018 (Morales 2019), while France has launched #NeRienLaisserPasser, the first online portal of its kind in the world – a 24-hour police-run chatline for reporting or talking about sexual assault or sexist discrimination (Willsher 2019).

17 The ad generated both praise and angry criticism (Topping *et al.* 2019).

18 Mention of #MeToo occurred a number of times in the Munk Debate 'Political correctness gone mad?', moderated by Rudyard Griffiths and featuring Stephen Fry, Jordan Peterson, Michael Eric Dyson, and Michelle Goldberg. Fry likened what he characterized as the mood in the wake of #MeToo of not being able to speak freely of sexual romantic feeling to 'it's like the Stasi listening: you'd better be careful' (Griffiths 2018: 82). But Goldberg argued that 'the idea that it's become this all-encompassing Stalinist inquisition' or that persons were ruined on the back of 'a McCarthyist rumour' was 'a bit of an exaggeration'. She pointed out that Bill Cosby had two trials and that there were 'any number of women telling similar stories of the most brutal sorts of rape', and that Weinstein lost his career 'only after being accused credibly and repeatedly with hard evidence of payouts by many, many women' (Griffiths 2018: 17).

19 Broadcaster Paul Gambaccini and singer Cliff Richard – both cleared of allegations of historical sexual assault – have recently backed a pressure group campaigning for the anonymity of those accused of sexual offences (*Telegraph* 2019).

20 A number of these have been consulted for the present volume, among them Popova (2019) and Sanyal (2019).

21 In her book, Greer refers to 'banal rape' (2018: 70) and states (oddly) that '[if] we are talking physical injuries, these are usually the consequence of the assault, not of the rape per se' (Greer 2018: 57). Given that Greer (2018: 1) defines rape as 'penetration of the vagina of an unwilling human female by the penis of a human male' it seems odd to distinguish firmly between rape (or forced sex) and assault. The two often go together.

22 See also Chapter 2, Note 36.

23 For the purposes of this volume 'the Bible' refers to the Hebrew Bible (or Old Testament) and the New Testament (or Greek Bible). There are also narratives of and allusions to sexual harassment and violence in other ancient Jewish and early Christian writings. A study of sexual violence and the Apocrypha, or deuterocanonical writings of the Roman Catholic and Eastern Orthodox churches, would, however, certainly be possible. Notable here is the book of Susanna (sometimes included in the book of Daniel). The kernel of the story concerns the beautiful and virtuous Susanna who is observed bathing by two lecherous elders. When they try to blackmail her into having sex with them, she refuses. Susanna is about to be put to death for promiscuity when the young Daniel interrupts and proves her innocence. For a study of the book of Susanna and its early interpretation see Schroeder (2007: 206–20).

24 Marcion was an important figure during the early formative period of Christianity. While the Church Fathers excommunicated Marcion, his theology rejecting the deity of the Hebrew Bible in favour of the Father of Christ remained influential.

25 On violence, including sexual violence, as inherent in the institution of slavery in the New Testament era, see Marchal (2011).

26 For a succinct summary with examples, see Matthews (2017) and her 'Violence in the New Testament' (No date).

27 Other commentators argue that such a reading can be inverted by stressing that divine love is revealed not 'in the suffering of crucifixion itself – which would be akin to reifying and glorifying such suffering' but in divine 'solidarity with those who suffer, and … [in] vindicating and [the] healing restoration of such persons' (Matthews 2017: 51; cf. the practical application of this in Tamar Campaign 2007).

28 Schüssler Fiorenza expresses much of her analysis of violence against women in the terminology she creates. The term 'kyriarchal' in the quotation on p. 21 is coined by her and in feminist theory is used to refer to systemic oppression. Her use of 'G★d' and 'the★logy' seeks to draw attention to and challenge androcentric terminology. Another neologism of hers is 'wo/men', which intends to signal

that not all women are the same but differ according to class, ethnicity, race, sexuality, religion, nation, and experience. The slash also reminds that there are marginalized men in the world, and were throughout history, who face oppressions and who are also categorized as not 'real' men.

(Matthews 2017: 34, n.9)

29 The codes stress submission and discipline (e.g. Ephesians 5:22; 6:4–5), as well as toleration of harsh treatment (1 Peter 2:18–3:1) but also proscribe harsh treatment (Colossians 3:19) and advise just treatment (Colossians 4:1). They might be characterized as ranging from passive-aggressive to very aggressive.

30 There is certainly some preoccupation with women who adorn themselves and are not suitably modest. This is evident both in the Hebrew Bible (e.g. Isaiah 3:16; Hosea 2:13) and in the New Testament (1 Peter 3:3; 1 Timothy 2:9; Revelation 17:4).

31 See especially the contributions in Hornsby and Stone (2011). As Stone (2011: 95) points out, the Bible 'prove[s] to be less secure, less "straight"-forward ... than those who make ... appeals [to it] imagine'.

32 For a fuller discussion see Hornsby 2014. Hornsby (2014: 326) also contends here, however, that '[h]eteronormativity is not in the text, waiting to be discovered; the interpreter, or reader, brings the assumption of heteronormativity to the text to justify heteronormativity'.

33 In this verse, from the victory song of Deborah and Barak, the female advisors to General Sisera's mother account for the soldiers' delay in returning from battle by saying that each man is enjoying a *racham rachamātayim*, literally, 'a womb or two' (not, as NRSV translates more coyly, 'a girl or two for every man'). Guest (2011: 35) proposes here the more crass and colloquial 'a cunt or two for every dick'. This translation captures the intentionally lewd force well, I think. Male dominance is asserted using a violent sexual image of post-conquest rape.

34 I am in agreement with Clines (see p. 20) that the use of the word 'marriage' in the context of the Hebrew Bible is mostly euphemistic. In this particular passage from Judges, relating the seizure of the young women, or girls, of Shiloh, the term is particularly blatantly objectionable – hence, the inverted commas.

35 Not least, because a comparable pattern is evident also in the #MeToo disclosures, with male-on-female violence outnumbering other binary combinations. There are some indications that male–male sexual abuse is also high. This is demonstrated in the acutely distressing findings of the Australian Royal Commission into Institutional Responses to Child Sexual Abuse. Of the 6,875 survivors of abuse whose experiences are analysed therein, the majority are male and suffered abuse as minors. The majority of perpetrators are male Catholic priests (Peters and Besley 2019: 459).

36 I discuss these matters more fully elsewhere (Stiebert 2016: 82, n.97, 93, n.12, and 95).

37 Some interpreters do argue differently that 'know' pertains not to carnal knowledge but to 'investigating' the visitors to Sodom. For a persuasive argument along these lines, see Bailey (2010). On 'know' pertaining to sexual intercourse see Gravett (2004: 284, n.16).

38 It does so unequivocally in the inculcations of Leviticus 18 and 20 (e.g. Leviticus 18:7–8; Leviticus 20:11).

39 For a full discussion see Stiebert (2016: 100–09). As explained here, one less often made counter-case is that Noah may have abused Ham.

40 More hints of sexually aggressive male-on-male behaviour have been identified in Ishmael's mocking of Isaac (Genesis 21:9) and the Philistines' demeaning humiliation of Samson – both times using verbs of the root *tsch-q* (Judges 16:25). This word designates sexual insult at Genesis 39:14 and 39:17. The Samson story also incorporates the verb *'nh* (Judges 16:5, 6, 19; cf. Gravett 2004: 295). For a fuller discussion see Stiebert (2019: 95–96, n.46). Others have also suggested Job 30:11 (Gravett 2004: 287–88), Jeremiah 20:7–8 (Crenshaw 1984: 39; Stone 2007) and Lamentations 3 (Nagouse 2018).

41 On sexualized abuse of Jesus see Tombs (1999) and on the New Testament affirmation of the ubiquitous and unexceptional abuse of slaves – including for sexual abuse – with particular reference to The Letter of Paul to Philemon, see Marchal (2011). As stated above, in the New Testament links between sexual violence and Christian theology are for the most part covert, as opposed to overt.

42 For a comprehensive discussion see Williams (1999). Williams argues that the main binary in Roman sexuality is conceived of not so much in terms of heterosexual/homosexual but of free/slave and dominant/subordinate.

43 This is reflected also of female slaves in the Hebrew Bible (see p. 27). As with boys in pederastic sex there is no indication with female slaves either of such notions as age of consent or statutory rape.

44 Like Hebrew words, Koine words are transliterated here. The word *doulos* is also used in the centurion's words that demonstrate his authority (Matthew 8:9; Luke 7:8).

45 For an example, see Jennings' chapter 'The Centurion's Lad' (2003: 131–44). For a revised and more nuanced version, see Jennings and Liew (2004).

46 Zeichmann is non-committal about whether the centurion and the slave have sex. As he points out, this is not made explicit in either telling of the Gospel story. His point is that a Roman slave cannot make free decisions, including concerning participation in sex acts with his master. The same appears to be the case with female slaves in certain Hebrew Bible passages (see p. 27).

47 Jael's murder of Sisera (Judges 4:18–21; 5:26–27) is also sometimes argued to constitute an aggressive quasi-sexual act, or reversed rape (see Stiebert 2016: 121–22 and 122, n.81). Another woman behaving in a sexually forward way towards a man and with destructive intent is the adulteress of Proverbs 7 (vv.21–23). See Note 40 above on the possibility that Delilah, alongside the Philistines, humiliates Samson sexually.

48 I have discussed this story and its implications fully elsewhere (Stiebert 2019).

49 The story is sparsely told and variously interpreted, with some commentators arguing that the narrative subverts events and projects Lot's desire on to his daughters. Others contend that the story is above all about trickery and overturning social norms, possibly for comic effect. Others again, see the story as celebrating female initiative. There is considerable disagreement as to whether the story, implicitly or otherwise, critiques Lot, the daughters, both, or neither. I have discussed these matters fully elsewhere (Stiebert 2016: 156–65).

50 Scholz (2010: 169) agrees: 'the male character is an unambiguous rape victim.'

51 I discuss the lack of and possible hints at female–female sexualization in the Hebrew Bible fully elsewhere (Stiebert 2016: 114–32).

52 Sarai and Abram are better known by their post-covenant names – Sarah and Abraham.

53 Hagar's disdain for Sarai is widely accounted for as deriving from Hagar's feeling of superiority – because she has conceived, whereas Sarai had not. As such, Sarai may be angered at what she considers Hagar's insubordination (see Stiebert 2019: 75, n.5). As Katie Edwards (private correspondence) points out, however, such a reason is not spelled out and Hagar might also – quite justifiably and understandably! – feel disdain on account of how inhumanely she has been treated. After all, Hagar is handed to Abram and is raped for the purpose of bearing a child that will not be hers (Genesis 16:1–2).

54 I have discussed this narrative more fully elsewhere (Stiebert 2013: 50–59).

55 The trope of the dangerous and sexually provocative foreign woman is well established in the Bible (see Stiebert 2019: 85–88 and Chapter 2 below).

56 Blyth (2010: 159) discusses the many interpretations that project onto Dinah's solo excursion 'pejorative overtones of sexual and social impropriety' but finds the biblical text itself free from such overtones, concluding that '[Dinah's] departure … has the appearance of a distinctly harmless act, devoid of any pejorative content … and … contextualized within the strictly gendered space of *female* companionship'. For analysis of numerous interpretations of the Dinah story, mostly from the early Church through to the Reformation and often demonstrating such overtones, see Schroeder (2007: 11–51).

57 Bechtel (1994: 29), instead, considers Amnon's feelings of hatred and loathing of his rape victim (2 Samuel 13:15, see p. 27) to be a more plausible and typical post-rape response. Keady, meanwhile, points out that persons who profess to love do rape. She cites a recent example of a man who abducted a woman, raped her and coerced her into marriage (Keady 2018: 69–70, 76).

58 See, for instance, Davies (2003: 56–57), Shemesh (2007: 2–21), Scholz (2000, 2010) – who specifies that this is an example of acquaintance rape (Scholz 2010: 32–38) – Klopper (2010), and, most fully, Blyth (2010). I also recommend Dube (2017) who reads Shechem as a rapist but as a rapist who, being cast as 'a native with uncontrolled sexual passions', 'does the unimaginable' (2017: 52) – namely, he is one of the colonized who rapes and then wants to marry a daughter of the colonizer. Dube's subtle reading is much informed by damaging discourses and experiences of conquest from her own southern African setting. Penner and Cates (2007: 37.2) also explore the colonizing interpretations of Genesis 34 and point out the silencing of the colonized Shechemites. Their interpretation, however, highlights above all the 'obscurity and ambiguity' of the narrative (Penner and Cates 2007: 37.5).

59 The allusion to the event in the apocryphal book of Judith also describes what looks like rape (Judith 9:2). The rape in turn leads on to revenge rape (Judith 9:4).

60 This short book remains a classic of feminist biblical interpretation. Scholz (2018: 185–86) rightly calls this a 'pioneering book … the first feminist-scholarly book ever published on sexual violence in the Bible'. The sole focus text that is not a rape text is Judges 11, the story of Jephthah's sacrifice

of his daughter. I disagree with Bal (1988: 64–65 and 68) that Jephthah's carrying out of the sacrifice of his daughter and shedding her blood inevitably conjures up a groom laying his virgin bride on the marriage bed before having sexual intercourse with her.

61 The Hebrew verb is of the root *znh* from which is derived the noun *zônâ*, meaning sex-worker but rendered in most translations as 'prostitute' (NRSV), 'harlot' (New American Standard), or 'whore' (King James Version [KJV]). The verb can refer to unfaithfulness or disobedience in matters other than those pertaining to sexual continence. The verb is accompanied by a preposition with pronominal suffix meaning 'against him'. Some translations have '[she] deserted (him)' (see Sefaria), which is legitimate, while others have 'she was unfaithful to him' (e.g. New International Version [NIV]). The Hebrew text is ambiguous as to whether the Levite's wife committed any sexual impropriety. This is also maintained in some English translations, such as the Douay-Reims Bible, which has 'she left him'. Other English translations, however, are judgement-laden. This is most blatant with the Jubilee Bible, which translates '[she] committed adultery against him'. See Bible Hub.

62 This interpretation is reflected in the New Living and Good News translations and goes back to the Greek of the Septuagint, which has *ōrgisthē auto*, 'she was angry with him'.

63 While the story is in many ways very sparsely told and avoids any personal names, there is here a clear shorthand to point out who the 'baddies' of the story are. The story also contains notable detail in terms of places or affiliations with place. Hence, there is mention of suspicion of 'foreigners' (Judges 19:12) and of being from Ephraim (Judges 19:1, 16, 18), or Bethlehem in Judah (Judges 19:1–2), or Gibeah (Judges 19:14, 16) and of being of the children of Israel (Judges 19:12). One reason for this may be that the rape ultimately leads to war among the tribes of Israel (Judges 20) – and then to more rape (Judges 21).

64 The similarity with Lot's offer to the thugs of Sodom to rape his two virgin daughters (Genesis 19:8) is clear and widely noted by commentators.

65 In her close reading of this text Trible (1984) discusses in detail how gynosadistic (that is, cruel and abhorrent about and for women) this story is.

66 Mercifully, this part of the story is not told with much elaboration. Two verbs describe the thugs' action: the first is from *yd'* ('they knew'), a verb sometimes used of carnal knowledge, or sexual intercourse, and used together with the signifier of the definite object – i.e. '(they knew/sexually abused) her'; the second is from *'ll* with the preposition 'in' and a pronominal suffix ('they thrust into her' or 'they severely abused her'). For more in-depth information on this verb, see Gravett (2004: 284). Later, when the Levite recounts events (Judges 20:5), he uses a verb from the root *'nh* applied to the men of Gibeah. Here '(my wife) they raped' (e.g. NIV) is an apt translation. Added to this is 'and she died', which is appropriately translated consequentially: 'so that she died' (e.g. New King James Version [NKJV]) or 'until she was dead' (New Living Translation). The International Standard Version captures the horror with 'they tortured … to death'. While detail is sparse, and no attempt is made to give insight into the wife's perspective, the account is of a woman who is brutally raped to death.

67 Trible's (1984) reading in her chapter entitled 'An Unnamed Woman: The Extravagance of Violence' makes the multiple levels on which the wife is violated particularly clear.

68 I have discussed 2 Samuel 13 more fully elsewhere (Stiebert 2013: 59–64, 2016: 182–93).

69 Verbs of the root *'nh* refer twice more to Amnon's rape of Tamar in later reflections (2 Samuel 13:22, 32).

70 This is clearly rape. Amnon refuses to listen to Tamar's protest. He overpowers her (Hebrew *yechezeq mimenneh*, literally 'he was stronger than her'), he rapes her (from *'nh*), and he 'lies with her' or, given that the verb 'to lie' has a direct object, the colloquial 'he laid her' is apt.

71 The vast majority of modern commentators, including Trible (1984), read 2 Samuel 13 as an affecting story of the violent rape of an obedient young woman. I have discussed Tamar as ideal rape victim elsewhere (Stiebert 2013: 61–64, 98). One glaring exception is Reis (1998) who interprets Tamar as a manipulative schemer seeking to marry the heir to the throne. I reject her interpretation and consider it toxic and victim-blaming (see Scholz 2010: 41; Stiebert 2016: 188–91). Schroeder points out that in early Church and medieval interpretation the story is often cast as a cautionary tale about predatory men who appear honourable on the surface. Moreover, Tamar is also sometimes reproached in interpretations from this earlier time, including for destroying her brothers (Schroeder 2007: 153–90).

72 As in contemporary times (see Introduction, Note 37) there is a suggestion in the Hebrew Bible of more and of less 'deserving' victims of rape. Hence, the narrator makes every effort to construct Amnon as a sly and nefarious villain who planned his violent deed, deceiving his father and the sister he ought to have protected and thereby abusing both his physical advantage and his social status, while Tamar is cast as an entirely innocent victim of evil connivance who could not have foreseen or resisted what befalls her. Tamar is 'a tragic heroine, beautiful, royal, virginal, obedient, courageous, and wise in the face of threat and violence; forces beyond her control conspire against her through no fault of her own, and she comes to harm' (Stiebert 2013: 64). Tamar is thereby portrayed in very sympathetic terms as an entirely respectable and innocent victim of rape, whereas other portrayals (such as those of the rapes of the Levite's wife and Dinah) leave some scope for questioning: after all, the Levite's wife 'played the harlot' (i.e. may have been unfaithful) and left her husband, and Dinah went to see the women of the land. Certainly some commentators have picked up on such elements to impute or allocate some suspicion and blame. Such narrative elements and such interpretations are indicative of rape culture (see Chapter 2).

73 In modern contexts where surrogacy services sometimes facilitate predominantly affluent persons from wealthy countries having children born by less affluent women based in often considerably poorer countries, the story of Sarai and Hagar has new and still distinctly disturbing resonances. IVF Group Surrogacy Services, for instance, which offers surrogacy in the Ukraine, points out the 'flexibility of Ukrainian contract law' and lists 'the human right to be a parent' (i.e. of the couple commissioning the surrogate arrangement) well before both the rights and the obligations of the surrogate mother (see IVF Group Surrogacy Services). The surrogacy market is alive and well in a number of countries, notably the USA, India, Thailand,

Ukraine, and Russia, as well as Mexico, Nepal, Poland, and Georgia. Costs associated with surrogacy range from US$45,000 to US$100,000, depending on country (Cheung 2014).

74 Such is brought out even more clearly, particularly regarding intersectional dimensions of abuse, in Weems' womanist reading (1988).

75 The application of the term 'rapable' can be confusing. I am using it here in the sense of 'perceived as available for rape' (cf. Washington 1998). Elsewhere the term is used differently. Hence, when Popova (2019: 34) writes that '[i]n US legal history ... women of color – black and indigenous women in particular – were not regarded as rapable', what she means is that rape of these women was not considered a crime, because they were not accorded autonomy or legal protection. This, as Popova explains, made them particularly vulnerable to sexual violence but exonerated their rapists. She also points out that certain marginalized groups, such as sex workers and women of colour, are still disproportionately vulnerable to sexual violence and less likely to have their cases taken up by either investigators or prosecutors (Popova 2019: 25–26). Gqola (2018 [2015]: 4–5) concurs: 'Making Black women *impossible* to rape does not mean making them *safe* against rape. It means quite the opposite: that Black women are safe to rape, that raping them does not count as harm and is therefore permissible.'

76 Whereas in Genesis 20:4 (cf. Genesis 26:10–11) sexual interference is explicitly denied, the text of Genesis 12 is suggestive of sex, or is, at the very least, ambiguous. It says here Sarai 'was taken' *(wattuqqach)* to Pharaoh's house (Genesis 12:15) and later Pharaoh says 'I took her for a wife' (Genesis 12:19) (cf. Introduction, Note 25). Some later texts, notably the Genesis Apocryphon, which was found among the Dead Sea Scrolls, are emphatically apologist and spell out that Sarai was untouched by Pharaoh.

77 Similarly, Isaac puts Rebekah at risk of sexual violation (Genesis 26).

78 Van Wolde (2002a: 535) claims that 'this text does not talk about rape, but about an accepted form of sexual intercourse'. I believe the text is more sinister in that it *does* talk about rape – and makes rape acceptable. As Washington (1998: 205–06) points out, the delaying of rape for one month (Deuteronomy 21:13) should not detract from the sexual violence of this law. For an especially powerful interpretation drawing out the ethnic dimensions in the theology of rape in both this law and in contemporary times, such as is brutally enacted by ISIS against Yazidi women, for instance, see Rey (2016).

79 I have discussed elsewhere that the metaphor of daughter Jerusalem as a woman raped during the fall of the city to Babylonian conquerors, depicts her as someone more sinned against than sinning, with the intention of arousing God's protection and pity (Stiebert 2013: 190–95).

80 While some commentators persist in not exploring this story's violent undercurrent or in reading the story of David and Bathsheba as a romance, Clines (2009 [1995]: 225–26) bluntly and – in my view incisively – states: 'sex [here] is essentially an expression of royal power, and ... much more like rape than love'. I do not agree with Schulte (2017) who (in my view, weirdly) determines that rape in the context of the Bible occurs only when the deity is absent and signals an upset in the covenantal relationship, usually in terms of compromise with 'foreign' values. By this measure Dinah, the Levite's wife, and David's daughter Tamar are raped. But because 'the deity

is present in divine name in the last word of the last verse of 2 Samuel 11' (Schulte 2017: 137) Bathsheba is not raped. Instead, (bizarrely) Bathsheba's 'proactive washing' is an act of 'self-sanctifying' (Schulte 2017: 139) demonstrating that, like Ruth, she is a foreigner transitioning to an insider with 'legitimacy as a queen mother for Israel' (Schulte 2017: 138). Schulte (2017: 139) states confidently, 'Bathsheba is not raped but sanctified'. The possible subtexts of such a reading are very disturbing – namely, that foreignness is dirty and unholy, that those who are raped are deserted by God, and that what looks like rape is really a holy exercise.

81 David's action displeases God (2 Samuel 11:27) but David nonetheless goes on to be remembered as a man after God's own heart (Acts 13:22; cf. 1 Samuel 13:14). God's displeasure at his own sons taking human women is less clear. The act is accounted for by human women's beauty (Genesis 6:2; cf. the retelling in 1 Enoch 7:1–2). In the verse following the rape is the divine determination to restrict human lifespans to 120 years (Genesis 6:3). While this could be considered a direct consequence and punishment, it is also noted that the offspring, called Nephilim, continue to exist and were heroes, warriors of renown (Genesis 6:4).

82 Scholz (2010: 72, 75) also identifies Reuben's sex with Bilhah (Genesis 35:22; 49:3–4), Rachel's slave, as rape expressive of power and competition. She proposes that Reuben rapes Bilhah either to avenge his mother Leah, who was less loved than Rachel, or to challenge his father, Jacob.

83 A possible exception is suggested in Laban's words to Jacob (Genesis 31:50). Here Laban, having caught up with Jacob, who fled his presence together with his two wives who are also Laban's daughters, makes a pact with his son-in-law in which he calls on God as his witness to ensure that Jacob not 'ill-treat' (Jewish Publication Society translation) his daughters or take other wives besides them. The word translated 'ill-treat' is from *'nh* and could, therefore, pertain particularly to sex that is unwanted or humiliates, that is, in this case, marital rape *(pace* Van Wolde 2002a: 534).

84 Marital rape refers to forced sexual intercourse with one's spouse. Since the latter part of the twentieth century (since 1991 in the case of the UK) it has been enshrined in many legal systems as a form of domestic violence and sexual abuse. Until then, there existed a marital exemption from rape laws. This was, in part, because marriage was widely regarded as constituting an act granting irrevocable consent and also because of coverture: the practice whereby on marriage a woman's legal rights were subsumed under her husband's. Scholz (2010: 91) also proposes that the sexual activity Abimelech observes Isaac inflicting on his wife Rebekah (Genesis 26:8) is malicious and suggestive of rape. The verb is from the root *ts-ch-q* and is used of unwanted sexual activity in Potiphar's wife's accusation of attempted rape (Genesis 39:14, 17).

85 The word used of Tamar is from the root *sh-m-m* and suggests desolation, horror, and ruin. The word used of Dinah is from the root *t-m-'* and suggests pollution.

86 The word 'grind' applies to the suffering of young men at Lamentations 5:13, which could conceivably refer to the sexual humiliation of males also (Gravett 2004: 295).

87 There are additional images of violence. Gomer/Israel is hedged in by thorns (Hosea 2:6[8]) and uncovered (Hosea 2:10[12]). Following punishment, God

does allure her back (Hosea 2:13–14[15–16]), an action that Weems (1995) aptly likens to that of a manipulative domestic abuser.

88 The so-called 'pornoprophetic debate' in biblical studies is centred on whether sexualized and violent woman metaphors reflect stereotypes that cause little or no harm to actual women, or negative biases and misogyny with the potential for harmful impact on real women, past and present. Robert P. Carroll is associated with the former (though see his commentary on Jeremiah 13 cited on p. 30) and Athalya Brenner with the latter position (see Brenner 1996).

89 As van Dijk-Hemmes (1995) points out, it is especially disturbing that the feminized cities are blamed for being sexually abused in their youth: the language – of having their breasts pressed and fondled – is in the passive voice but nevertheless equated with whoredom (Ezekiel 23:3).

90 Similarly, the punishment of Jerusalem is again depicted in rape imagery through the depiction of the lifting up of skirts and violation (Jeremiah 20:22). Again, it is God who is cast as rapist (Jeremiah 20:26; cf. Nahum 3:5–6, of the punishment of Nineveh). It is also God who punishes the daughters of Zion by laying them bare (Isaiah 3:17).

91 Stories of Jezebel are to be found in the Hebrew Bible's Books of Kings. She is described as turning Ahab away from the worship of Israel's God and as promoting instead worship of the deities Baal and Asherah. Jezebel also persecuted the prophets of God (1 Kings 18) and fabricated evidence in a charge of blasphemy against Naboth (1 Kings 21), an innocent landowner, who had not wanted to sell his ancestral land to Ahab.

92 For a full analysis see Marshall (2009) and Glancy and Moore (2011).

93 Leviticus 18:22 and 20:13 both prohibit some form of sexual contact between two males, designating it an abomination. Most probably, penetrative sex is at issue. The latter verse again prescribes the death penalty for both parties. Again, the possibility of rape is not cited as an exemption.

94 In Judges 21 the men of Benjamin are instructed to take for themselves wives from among the maidens of Shiloh as they come out for harvest dances in the vineyards. The verb here for seizing, or abducting a woman is *nś'* (Judges 21:21, 23). Because the same verb is used in the book of Ruth when Naomi's sons 'take' Moabite wives (Ruth 1:4), Gafney (2009) has proposed that Orpah and Ruth, too, were abducted in rape marriage.

95 On violence in Song of Songs, see Fischer (2009).

96 The word sometimes translated 'molest' is from *ng'* ('to touch', cf. Genesis 26:29).

2 Rape culture, rape myths, and the Bible

Having established that gendered sexual violence is, first, increasingly reported in our own time, with #MeToo constituting something of a watershed, and, second, widely present in the Bible, let me next explore some ways to bring disparate texts and contexts into one viewing frame. In doing so, I will go on to introduce two more concepts: rape culture and rape myths. After setting the scene – with some qualifications and reasons for bringing together two sets of texts, ancient and contemporary – these concepts will become the focus.

Viewing the Bible and #MeToo bifocally: some considerations

There are both pronounced differences and points of pronounced affinity between, on the one hand, texts of gendered sexual violence in the Bible and, on the other, the revelations of #MeToo. In order to bring the two together, it is important both to highlight and qualify differences and affinities.

First, the relationship between texts and the contexts in which they arise is neither arbitrary, nor entirely straightforward. This is true both of ancient, including biblical, and of contemporary texts. Neither can be used like a mirror to make claims about capturing the social realities in which they arise: this is called 'the referential fallacy' (Pippin 1996: 52). What the Bible says is not likely to be an accurate representation of what 'biblical times' (whatever times in a large temporal spectrum these may be) were actually like. Even where biblical texts purport to recount historical events, it cannot be assumed that authors produced or audiences expected (only) factual and precisely recorded accounts. Biblical texts are infused by ideologies and this applies also to biblical rape texts.

Public texts of our own time, just like the biblical texts, do not reflect social realities completely accurately. By this I do *not* mean, with regard to #MeToo, that the movement has served to exaggerate and distort the extent and scale of sexual abusiveness, as is sometimes claimed.[1] Rather, the steep increase in both public declarations and in reports of sexual violence cannot be taken to indicate a sudden increase in sexual violation. Likewise, fewer instances of publicly declaring or of reporting sexual violence in times past cannot be taken to be indicative of fewer cases of sexual violence. There is much that actually mandates against this: most loudly of all, the flood of historical cases of sexual abuse, which indicates that in times past when comparatively few instances of sexual violence were reported, they nevertheless occurred in considerable number.[2] Even with some prominent individual #MeToo cases – notably, those of Harvey Weinstein (Farrow 2017; Kantor and Twohey 2017) and Charlie Rose (Brittain and Carmon 2018) – accusations date back decades before the onset of #MeToo.

David Clines (2009 [1995]) brilliantly applies Fredric Jameson's (1981) important findings on narrative and class to biblical texts and gender relations.[3] As both Clines and Jameson point out, texts are most often products, made for circulation and for the consumption of a readership and a market. For Jameson, *all* texts owe their existence to a desire to repress social conflict, 'to make life easier for the oppressors and the oppressed, to allow the oppressors to deny their role and to enable the oppressed to forget their suffering' (Clines 2009 [1995]: 101). Certainly the earliest texts of #MeToo, such as tweets, are rather different from biblical texts: notably, in terms of their short, topical, and predominantly ephemeral intentionality. Still, the movement appears to have proliferated and to have generated sustained impact through streams of responses and texts, because it arrived at a time appropriate to the demands or interests of the consuming audiences. In terms of the social conflict that the movement addresses, persistent gender inequality seems to be the obvious contender. The movement can be said to help the oppressed – that is, victims of sexual abusiveness – by giving them a forum and a sense of solidarity through the creation of and connection with an online community of support.[4] It could also be said to help the oppressor, that is, perpetrators of sexual abusiveness: first, through the creation of such a vast deluge of revelations that abusiveness (albeit unintentionally) becomes less shocking, even more normalized and also easier to dismiss as either 'exaggeration' or 'the way things are'; or, second, through creating a few 'monsters' – such as Harvey Weinstein, for example, whose abuses have been reported in so much detail as to verge on the grotesque – so that it becomes easier for the more 'regular variety' of abuser to fade from view, given that they are 'not *that* bad' in comparison.

While social tensions may be in the background of the shared emphasis on gender-based violence in biblical texts and #MeToo there is an important difference between them both in terms of *who gets to speak* and *how sexual violence is spoken of*. The rape of Tamar (2 Samuel 13),[5] for instance, is constructed with chronology and consequence in mind (and is in that sense 'historical'): it is a narrative determined by prior events (David's rape of and adultery with Bathsheba and the murder of her husband Uriah in 2 Samuel 11) and which sets in motion subsequent events, namely, the murder of Amnon (2 Samuel 13:28–32) and Absalom's rape of and adultery with David's wives (2 Samuel 16:20–22). Insofar as the account is historical, this is very much theologized[6] history: hence, punishment is depicted as occurring on account of divine displeasure (2 Samuel 11:27), which is communicated by Nathan, the court prophet, relaying YHWH's[7] words (2 Samuel 12:7–14). While the literary characters may represent historical figures,[8] the account clearly contains narrative invention. Hence, the rape occurs with only Amnon and Tamar present (2 Samuel 13:9) and there is no suggestion that either wrote or directly informed the narrative – yet there is a vivid and detailed account of the rape, inclusive of direct dialogue (2 Samuel 13:10–16). This is transparently the work of an inventive narrator, and not a witness account. And Tamar, while vividly, though briefly, portrayed, is best understood as a literary character and, therefore, a literary victim of rape.[9] Whether the rape actually happened or not, this is a literary rape where Tamar is *spoken about* in a text that is responding to social tensions.

Thus, the narrator of 2 Samuel 13 makes every appearance of being sympathetic to Tamar – by depicting her as an innocent victim overpowered by a deceitful man who ought to have protected, not violated, her – but it is uncertain how reliable the narrator is. As Danna Nolan Fewell and David Gunn point out, in biblical texts 'women's experience has been rewritten – fictionalized and idealized from an androcentric point of view' and this means that on the subject of a woman's rape, biblical narrators 'can never be wholly reliable' (Fewell and Gunn 1993: 82).

For all this lack of reliable and first-hand information, it can be said that Tamar is more articulate than other biblical rape victims, because not only is her performative communication (2 Samuel 13:19)[10] narrated but also her spoken words (2 Samuel 13:12–13, 16). This is not the case with other literary rape victims in the Bible. Consequently, there is little else to go on in terms of how the experience of rape trauma was understood. What *is* there indicates that rape was understood to be violent, shaming, defiling, destructive – but what is lacking is the perspective of rape victims. With Dinah, for instance, as Blyth (2010: 4) writes,

> [t]here is a pervasive narrative silence about this character's personal experience of sexual violence and a denial of, or at least a contextual lack of interest in, the fact that Shechem's act of sexual assault was a forcible violation of her bodily integrity and that it would have been a source of immense physical, emotional and spiritual distress for her.

Indeed, a lot has been lost in the mists of time and in (ill-understood) transmission and redaction processes. We cannot establish, for example, who wrote the biblical texts, or exactly when, where, or why. Authorial identification or intention remains guesswork. What is, however, revealing in terms of authors' and transmitters' purposes and interests[11] is what texts do say, what they omit, and what they assume. As Clines (2009 [1995]: 95, italics in original) distinguishes judiciously in his examination of the ideologies of texts, the focus needs to shift to identifying

> the *implied* author and the *implied* social setting of the text—to draw inferences … not to attempt a move from the text to the historical actuality that generated the text, but rather to sketch the kind of historical matrix the text implies.

Hence, the inference in both Genesis 34 and 2 Samuel 13 is that what matters in the stories of Dinah's or Tamar's rape is not the victim's trauma or violation but how rape incites honour conflicts between men. If we add to this the casual mention of raped women during war – such as in the legal codes and prophetic texts – what this communicates audibly is how rape is likely to have been regarded in the social contexts in which these texts were written and transmitted. Dinah's emotional experience of rape is completely passed over and even in Tamar's story emphasis comes to rest instead on male feelings of anger, vengefulness, and vindication, suggesting that these matter more, or are more interesting to the implied readership. The impact of rape on victims is rendered virtually irrelevant. In accounts of war, meanwhile, rape is normalized. Similarly, the use of the word 'rape' in colloquial speech in our own time,[12] alongside the prevalence of rape 'jokes' and rape myths, are, as I will go on to discuss, indicative of rape culture where sexual violence is, likewise, widely trivialized and casualized.

One very pronounced difference between the Bible's narratives and #MeToo texts, then, is that #MeToo gives voice and a forum for disclosure to those who have been harassed, abused, or raped. This is particularly immediate in the Facebook posts, blog posts, tweets and first-person accounts that disclose experiences of sexual abuse and rape. At one remove, very many reports and analyses centred on #MeToo also offer representation of and sometimes direct quotations from victims. This is not the case with biblical texts where victims of sexual abuse are only ever *written about*.[13] While normalization of sexual violence is in evidence in both biblical and contemporary contexts, #MeToo gives voice and some autonomy to victims where the biblical text does not.

A point of similarity – which again requires some qualification – is that in respect of both the ancient texts of the Bible and present-day texts, those that receive the most circulation and prominence tend to be by dominant and socially as well as economically advantaged groups in society. With the Bible this has been demonstrated persuasively by numerous commentators who point out that the very production of written texts, as well as literacy itself, is likely to have been for most of antiquity the exclusive preserve of affluent social elites. Moreover, Clines (2009 [1995]) points out repeatedly how the constituent texts of the Bible reflect the interests and preoccupations of the wealthy strata of society. As Robert Carroll (1997 [1991]: 79) too, states bluntly, '[w]hat the Bible (either testament and any version) represents is not what ancient peoples thought and did but what élites among ancient peoples wrote and tried (perhaps successfully) to impose by way of ideological control.'

In respect of #MeToo, it can be said, on the one hand, that the internet has democratized access to information, as well as the making or generating of information. Certainly, the bulk of those who contributed to the 'digitally mediated consciousness raising'[14] that is #MeToo are not famous and not ostensibly powerful individuals. And yet, as already discussed, in terms of broader systemic patterns, the fact remains that the majority of #MeToo participants are from the West.[15] Also, while burgeoning movements have gathered momentum elsewhere – in India, Pakistan, Thailand, and Egypt, for instance – there remains a discrepancy between where sexual violence is particularly prevalent and where forums such as #MeToo are centred (see Hargreaves 2018).[16] This can be explained in part in terms of lack of access in much of the Two-Thirds world to technology and the internet. Yet even in regions where digital literacy and access are commonplace, more systemically empowered groups (notably, privileged white women) receive more publicity and more attention in #MeToo, as well as in subsequent reports. And this in spite of the movement's roots in

Black activism (Hill 2017) and in spite of the disproportionate vulnerability to sexual harassment and abuse of less socially empowered groups, among these, persons of colour, those with disabilities, and members of the LGBT community.[17] Matters of power remain significant for determining whose demands receive a sizable forum, publicity, and visibility.

In summary, among the pronounced *differences* between both sets of texts are:

- Much about the contexts in which biblical texts emerged and in which they functioned is uncertain, whereas the emergence and impact of #MeToo is recorded and observable.
- Biblical texts describe sexual violence but offer no access or direct insight into the experience of victims, whereas #MeToo offers first-person and direct accounts from numerous victims of sexual harassment and violence.
- While not all parts of the Bible are equally well known and biblical texts of violence are among those least likely to be read out in public or to form the kernel of a sermon,[18] what is recorded in the Bible has been canonized and consulted for centuries: hence, the texts of the Bible have gravitas and have stood the test of time. The tweets, posts, and reports about #MeToo have demonstrated collective efficacy and, two years on, momentum continues, but #MeToo might be largely of its time, with its long-term impact still uncertain.[19]

Among the *similarities* between both sets of texts are:

- Both emerged in response to particular settings and demands and reflect social conflicts that incorporate gendered dimensions.
- Both reflect some considerable degree of preoccupation with sexual violence.
- In both, sexual violence is most often perpetrated by men against women – although not to the exclusion of mention of other gendered dynamics.
- In both, who speaks and whose interests are represented reveals much about who has more power.
- Those with least power are unrepresented (or, at best, acutely under-represented).

Without eliding distinctions between ancient and modern texts, both reflect the violence of the power dynamics that underlie them. As

Gravett (2004: 298) points out, '[w]omen and men in [the biblical] cultural settings might not understand or process their experiences in the same way as twenty-first-century persons endure rape and all of its repercussions.' But there do appear to be links and some common reactions in both settings, which she distils in terms of 'the sense of physical violation, the feelings of shame and being outcast, the loss of self and place in the culture – however different the reasons for such responses' (Gravett 2004: 298). And this, in turn can motivate, she continues, 'an act of political resistance to ideologies dominant in the biblical period', because the text is, through the establishment of such connections, opened up 'beyond the bounds set thousands of years ago ... [inviting us] to be more than passive recipients of ancient words – and to do more than simply reinscribe the cultural norms of these past societies onto the modern stage' (Gravett 2004: 298).

The reasons for discussing the two groups of texts together are various but are aimed in the first instance, at coming to understand more fully one topic they share and which connects them – namely, gendered sexual violence. I am not claiming that the Bible, while the biggest bestseller of all time, is the only, or even the major, source of the global and very high rates of sexual violence. I do, however, echo the contention that the Bible 'must be interrogated as a text that both supports and perpetuates such violence ... [because] we cannot afford to ignore the potential for biblical traditions to contribute to the harm experienced by countless victims of gender violence' (Colgan and Blyth 2018: 203).

Biblical texts are compelling. They have been around and have been pored over, consulted, and interpreted for centuries, right up to the present. Not only in Bible-using faith communities but also in wider, including popular, culture, biblical texts are part of the fabric of many human communities – including my own. They are, consequently, not only ancient repositories but also shapers of contemporary discourses and of meaning. Due to the authority and ubiquity of the Bible the impact of biblical gender violence extends beyond words on pages and 'continue[s] to have power in contemporary communities to sustain rape-supportive discourses' (Colgan and Blyth 2018: 204). This, as I am about to elucidate, is at the heart of rape culture.

Notwithstanding that modern readers of the Bible may recognize points of continuity and of affinity across a large span of time, there is also much in biblical texts that is unfamiliar, hard to make sense of, or that conflicts with contemporary sensibilities and attitudes.[20] It is best to admit to gaps in knowledge, disconnects, and puzzlement. I am suspicious of approaches that make strong claims to such things as 'authorial', 'real', 'original', or 'biblical' meaning. Unearthing, or retrieving such meaning in any pristine form is impossible – because we do not know what the original context or provenance of biblical texts is and because we lack reliable historical information about 'the biblical period'. In addition, our present context invariably affects meaning-making. I agree with Scholz (2005: 36.2) that 'readers create textual meaning even when they claim to reiterate only positions of the original writers'. This is because the reader's choice of texts and the circumstances that shape their choices and interpretations are ever present – whether a reader is conscious of this or not.

Meaning is dynamically created and recreated. As biblical texts move through time and varied contexts, different processes of meaning-making come to bear on them. It is no accident that social and political movements, as they arise and exert influence, come also to manifest in interpretations of the Bible. Hence, first-wave feminism gave rise to *The Woman's Bible* (1895–98); second-wave feminism gave rise to a flourish of feminist biblical criticism; oppressive regimes and movements for liberation in Latin America gave rise to biblical liberation theology – and so forth. This book makes the case that #MeToo brings fillips for reflection and meaning-making to the interpretation of biblical texts of sexual violence. This will, in turn, I hope, lead on to critically informed understanding of the influence of the Bible on rape cultures of our time and, subsequently, to effective and active resistance to the toxic texts and interpretations that contribute to sustaining rape cultures.

Foundations for this kind of investigation are already there in biblical studies. Since the 1980s, from which time second-wave feminism became firmly rooted in biblical studies, the study of sexual violence in the Bible has been steadily present (see Scholz 2018: 185–86). Phyllis Trible's *Texts of Terror* (1984) was a watershed.[21] Other feminist commentators went on to follow Trible's lead; early among them were Cheryl J. Exum and Renita Weems.[22] It is since 2000, however, that 'the flood waters have broken in biblical studies, and comprehensive and detailed investigations have consistently appeared on the topic of sexual violence and rape in biblical literature' (Scholz 2018: 187).[23]

More specifically, the topic of rape culture is also making inroads in biblical studies. The designation 'rape culture' has existed since the 1970s but has come into wide circulation in mainstream sources only since the second decade of the twenty-first century (Phillips 2017: 14–17). It appears only occasionally in biblical studies prior to this time, with Harold Washington (1998) being an early user. But very recently, even prior to #MeToo, the designation moved more to the fore here too (e.g. Kalmanofsky 2017: 17–20). The three-volume anthology *Rape*

Culture, Gender Violence, & Religion, edited by Caroline Blyth, Emily Colgan, and Katie B. Edwards (2018) includes one volume on biblical perspectives and also (just) predates #MeToo. The movement itself also found rapid response and resonance both in biblical studies[24] and in religious communities. An example of the latter is the hashtag #ChurchToo, launched by Twitter users Hannah Paasch and Emily Joy to prompt the sharing of stories of sexual abuse in church settings (Quackenbush 2017).[25]

Digressing for a moment, let me focus briefly on biblical studies and why an investigation like this one, on the Bible and #MeToo, fits into the discipline as it has been reconfigured in many academic institutions in recent years. It is undeniable that in England certainly (though not in England alone) biblical studies has suffered a significant downturn. The reason has less to do with a decline in interest in religion, the Bible, or biblical literacy[26] and more with a hammering of humanities subjects more generally. Hence, in 2010, when this was already well under way, the then Universities Minister David Willetts announced that degree courses in the arts, humanities, and social sciences at England's universities would phase out teaching grants (Richardson 2010). This was preceded by patterns of phasing out whole humanities disciplines in numerous universities (with languages particularly significantly affected) and investing instead in subjects such as sports science and media studies that met student demand (see Lipsett 2009). This demand, in turn, was in large part generated by the sharp increase of university tuition fees, which saw the entrenchment of consumer-driven models of education (Brown and Carasso 2013).[27] Consequently, student demand has come to drive course offerings and academic disciplines have had to justify their existence in terms of yielding returns on investment, such as in terms of how the dis-cipline develops skills desirable in the employment market. Universities are, quite simply, in competition with each other for students who, in England, pay up to £9,250 annually for an undergraduate degree.

Biblical studies has traditionally focused on the study of ancient lan-guages (notably, Biblical Hebrew, Biblical Aramaic, and Koine Greek), as well as on textual and historical criticism. In times past, this was often supplemented with the study of ancient languages additional to those of the Bible (e.g. Ugaritic, Egyptian, Mesopotamian Aramaic, Akkadian), as well as, often, the study of modern languages in order to read archae-ological reports (often in French) and the interpretations and commen-taries by notable scholars based in Germany or the Netherlands, among other centres of learning. Programmes in England that could offer such training in numerous ancient and modern languages, alongside textual criticism and biblical history, are now confined to very few universities indeed, with the elite institutions of Oxford and Cambridge by far the best staffed and resourced to offer these.

What has tended to happen, particularly outside of these few centres of learning, is that biblical studies has become less stand-alone and more absorbed into programmes of theology or religious studies. Hence, there may be modules in the discipline taught here and there, or study of the Bible might feature as part of a module on sacred texts or world literature. Much about this state of affairs is lamentable. But – for the topic of focus here – there is something of a (thin) silver lining. This is because the study of the Bible has had to – for its very survival – reinvent itself in the majority of university settings. It has had to become more interdisciplinary, more receptive to the demands of young students and to the popular media that inform them. And it is precisely these kinds of factors that have created a space for explorations such as this one, which interfaces skills and texts of the biblical studies tradition (such as close scrutiny of ancient texts)[28] with the recent and resonating media-driven phenomenon that is #MeToo.

Also, moving beyond the primary focus of investigating and better understanding sexual violence, both in the Bible and in the present, this study hopes to promote informed feminist advocacy – that is, active resistance to how texts contribute to the perpetuation of rape culture and gender violence. As Scholz argues, this seeks to buck 'academia's general reticence to address sexual violence' or what she calls 'a "cop-out" hermeneutics' (Scholz 2018: 181). Protest holds a continual presence in universities. This was in evidence, for instance, in recent mass strikes in the UK, in which academic staff and students often joined forces.[29] Moreover, it speaks to the growing rise of mass protest movements using social media in their tool-kit of mobilization – mass movements which include but also extend well beyond universities. #MeToo, targeting endemic sexual harassment, exploitation, and violence, is just one such movement. Others have preceded and followed, such as Occupy[30] and Extinction Rebellion.[31] Not to be underestimated in all of these movements is the significant intersection with religion[32] – as this book illustrates with reference to the Bible and #MeToo.

Before proceeding with efforts towards active feminist resistance, let me mention that, interestingly, the Bible has also featured in the popular press in the backlash to #MeToo. This should not surprise. The Bible is far from internally consistent[33] and lends itself to prooftexting – that is, to cherry-picking verses or passages and using these outside of their context to argue a particular position.[34] A recent example, where the Bible was deployed to discredit allegations of sexual harassment and assault, concerns the hearings for then Supreme Court nominee Brett

Kavanaugh (who has since been confirmed as a judge). In the course of these hearings, Kavanaugh was plausibly accused of historical sexual assault by Dr Christine Blasey-Ford. Some of Kavanaugh's supporters used the story of Joseph and Potiphar's wife in Genesis 39 as their rallying cry to discredit Blasey-Ford. In many public tweets, Kavanaugh was likened to Joseph and Blasey-Ford to Potiphar's wife. Analogously, Kavanaugh's election – like Joseph's eventual restoration and elevation to high office – was seen as a triumph for God's plan.[35] This is one example of how the Bible is utilized in the present to promote rape culture. Rape culture will be my next topic of focus.

Rape culture

Susan Brownmiller's important feminist[36] monograph on rape, *Against Our Will* (1975),[37] has been instrumental in determining at least three points about rape that have come to be widely accepted. The first is that rape is not rare and that it does not derive principally from sexual attraction but, instead, from a desire to dominate, intimidate, and control. Second, Brownmiller's book validates the perspectives of rape victims as well as their accounts that rape causes considerable and long-term harm and trauma.[38] And third, Brownmiller demonstrates that rape is not only common but is underpinned and fostered by, as well as indicative of, misogyny and sexism that is much more widespread and that manifests in ways that are both subtle and glaring. It is especially the latter, the notion that sexual violence is sustained and enabled by a wider environment that permits and normalizes such violence, that gets to the heart of what rape culture is.

In the same year as the publication of Brownmiller's book, the documentary *Rape Culture* (1975) was released, indicating that the concept of the film's title was beginning to gain circulation.[39] The designation 'rape culture', therefore, originated in the second-wave feminist movement of the 1970s to describe how sexualized violence, targeted particularly against women, had become normalized. It did not, however, gain wide traction until the second decade of the twenty-first century. As illustrated by Nickie Phillips (2017: 3), 'use of the term skyrocketed in 2013'. Phillips' collation of the frequency of the term in scholarly sources demonstrates a spike after 1994, 'indicating solid academic acceptance', and much increased occurrence since 2010. In mainstream sources, meanwhile, the spike is not pronounced until 2010–14 and in Google trends not until 2013 (Phillips 2017: 14–17).

What 'rape culture' refers to is a cultural milieu and context that in various ways facilitates rape-supportive environments and, consequently, the occurrence of sexual violence. The preamble to the revised edition of *Transforming a Rape Culture* (2005) describes this more fully as follows:

> [Rape culture] is a complex of beliefs that encourages male sexual aggression and supports violence against women. It is a society where violence is seen as sexy and sexuality as violent. In a rape culture, women perceive *a continuum of threatened violence* that ranges from sexual remarks to sexual touching to rape itself. A rape culture condones physical and emotional terrorism[40] against women and presents it as the norm.
>
> In a rape culture, both men and women assume that sexual violence is a fact of life, as inevitable as death or taxes. This violence, however, is neither biologically nor divinely ordained. Much of what we accept as inevitable is in fact the expression of values and attitudes that can change.
>
> (Buchwald *et al.* 2005: xi, emphasis added)

A somewhat similar but more concise definition is offered by Milena Popova: 'Rape culture is the collection of ideas, practices and structures in our society that make it easy for perpetrators to commit sexual violence and make it hard for victims to speak out or get justice' (Popova 2019: 4).

Such definitions are sometimes nuanced, to acknowledge more explicitly that men and transgender persons are also victims and women are perpetrators too, alongside recognizing that certain marginalized groups are especially vulnerable in rape cultures (e.g. Harding 2015: 2–5; Popova 2019: 26–27).[41] Still, the disproportionate victimization of females and feminized persons[42] is none the less widely acknowledged (Harding 2015: 5).[43] The other point in the definition by Buchwald *et al.* (2005) cited above, about the possibility of changing or reprogramming a rape culture, is acknowledged even by feminists such as Sanyal who downplay the influence of popular culture (e.g. of sexist lyrics) in terms of its power to shape gendered attitudes. Sanyal (2019: 110) concedes: 'Rape doesn't happen in a vacuum and isn't predestined genetically, but can be promoted or diminished – like all cultural acts – by cultural messages and norms. ... There are cultural scripts that promote rape and others that oppose it.' Others argue that examples from popular culture, or comments by influential individuals, even if 'seemingly trivial, can deeply influence our ideas about sexual violence' (Phillips 2017: 4). This is not, Phillips (2017: 155) argues, a case of 'carelessly labeling everything "rape" but instead is recognition that patterns of behavior rest on a continuum of sexual violence'.[44]

The rape culture continuum mentioned by Phillips is particularly aptly captured in a graphic model entitled 'rape culture pyramid'. The pyramid is published by the activist group '11th Principle: Consent!'. This group was formed in late 2012 following widely publicized sexual assaults at Burning Man, an annual summer event at Black Rock City (USA) that is an experiment in community and art. Burning Man is founded on ten main principles (among these are radical self-expression and civic responsibility). In 2012 the eleventh principle of informed consent was added. The pyramid model explains the structure of rape culture by beginning with the broad, yellow-coloured base of the pyramid, which lists microaggressions such as sexist attitudes, rape 'jokes', and locker room banter. It then moves upwards towards increasingly more orange stages, which include groping, revenge porn, and victim blaming and shaming, to the acutely red apex of rape. An arrow moves upwards along the rising edge from 'normalization' to 'degradation' to 'assault'. The point of this is to show in striking visual form that rape is founded on and shored up by a wide range of behaviours, which collectively constitute rape culture.

This rape culture gradation and continuum, illustrating how sexual assault is not far removed from widely normalized behaviours, might help to explain why rape, while typically criminalized and condemned, also remains fairly common. Hence, in the UK, rape carries a maximum penalty of life imprisonment,[45] indicating the seriousness of the crime, but the estimated occurrence of rape is approximately 85,000 rapes of women and 12,000 rapes of men annually in England and Wales.[46] Of these rapes, relatively few are reported and far fewer still transpire in court cases, let alone in convictions. Those who accept the existence of rape culture argue that rape continues to happen and continues to be suppressed, as opposed to being more and more widely reported and eventually ceasing to exist, because of endemic societal attitudes to gender and sexuality. Particularly at the level of microaggressions, these attitudes contribute to trivializing and normalizing sexual misconduct.

A number of variations of the rape culture pyramid have been created, with some versions listing different gradations of rape, citing 'incest' or 'gang rape', for instance, at the apex. These variations seem to suggest that certain rapes are worse than others (e.g. that incestuous rape is worse than non-incestuous rape, rape of children is worse than rape of adults, stranger rape is worse than date rape, rape of men is worse than rape of women, etc.),[47] or that 'there are "mild" rapes and "brutal" rapes, terrible but "understandable" rapes versus inexplicable and inexcusable rapes' (Gqola 2018 [2015]: 8), while others refute such a 'hierarchy'. Pumla Gqola, for instance, rejects all forms of gradation and concludes succinctly, 'All rape is brutal' (Gqola 2018 [2015]: 8). The argument that rape of attractive women is somehow more understandable, Gqola (2018 [2015]: 8) elaborates, rests on patriarchal assumptions about the 'symbolic availability of all women to male heterosexual pleasure' and determines that the act is still brutal and still inexcusable. 'Rape is never mild, never minor, never acceptable' (Gqola 2018 [2015]: 12).[48]

Not only is rape widely depicted in ways that imply gradations of severity,[49] there are also suggestions that victims experience rape differently. I can accept that victims of rape respond to and process their experience in different ways – this only makes sense, given that victims of rape are not only very, very numerous but a diverse group (including in terms of age, cultural and religious background, gender identity, socio-economic status, ability, education, life experience, relationship status, and so forth, not to mention individual personality). Added to this, victims are situated in contexts with diverse social expectations and they encounter different levels and structures of support – or none – from family, friends, medical and legal services, and so on. I can agree with Sanyal that some groups[50] and some individuals may well depart from what Vanessa Veselka (1998) deems the sole accepted 'script' for a female rape or abuse victim: that of the 'collapsible woman' who feels defiled, traumatized, destroyed. Some rape victims *are* destroyed by rape.[51] Some rape victims may feel neither destroyed, nor experience post-traumatic stress disorder (PTSD) and may not want either counselling or to report their rapist. But this does not mean that rape is not experienced by them as painful or life-changing.[52]

In acknowledgment of there being no one or 'right' response to rape, emergency rape support service providers in the UK report a range of responses from victims[53] and do not put pressure on rape victims to follow any one particular path (such as disclosing the rapist's identity or reporting the perpetrator to the police), instead taking the lead from the victim.[54] While there is no 'script', the bulk of evidence, from clinical studies, victim support groups, victim statements, and other sources testifies to the harm rape causes – in both the short and the long term. I am unconvinced that rape ever brings no harm at all to its victim (*pace* Greer, see p. 19) but I accept that it is impossible to make a blanket statement about a crime that is different in every case. I neither want to categorize rapes in terms of some being worse than others (how could this even be measured?), nor do I want to prescribe how traumatized rape victims should feel, or how they should respond and behave and act.[55] I am taking all rapes to be experienced as to some degree distressing and life-changing – because I see no persuasive evidence to the contrary.

Let me mention, however, that there is also resistance to the notion and designation of rape culture. There are vociferous rape culture deniers – such as Wendy McElroy, Luke Gittos, Camille Paglia, and Christina Marie Hoff Sommers – who claim that certainly in Western contexts the very notion is – in Paglia's word – 'ridiculous'.[56] More moderate thinkers, too, point out that the designation 'rape culture' covers such a wide phenomenological and social range as, arguably, to deplete it of meaning. Hence, the term is applied to vastly different places spanning from India – recently designated the most dangerous nation to be a woman, due to high risks of sexual violence, human trafficking, forced marriage, and sexual slavery, among other reasons – to Denmark, which rates consistently highly in terms of human rights and gender equality (Krishnan 2018). Bradley Campbell and Jason Manning ask, 'If the United States is a rape culture, then what about societies where some women receive no protection from rape at all? ... And which times and places are *not* rape cultures?' (Campbell and Manning 2018: 128–29). In response to this, it can be argued that language always poses confines. Words conjure different denotations and connotations for different persons and words change over time. Many words – including 'marriage', 'motherhood', 'religion', or 'rape' – mean different things to different people, different things in different contexts, and carry different associations through the passage of time. *All* language is located in particular historical, social, political, economic, and cultural environments, which makes this inevitable. The designation 'rape culture' does mean different things in India or Denmark or the USA, prison or war-zone settings, and so forth. It may well be true that *all* cultures are rape cultures to some degree.[57]

Peggy Reeves Sanday (2003), for instance, speaks of a spectrum ranging from 'rape-free' to 'rape-prone' societies, with societies fostering equality (particularly gender and social equality) and opportunities for participation, alongside an emphasis on individuals acquiring empathy and a developed self-understanding, evidencing lower rates of sexual and other violence. What this adds up to is not that 'rape culture' is a designation devoid of meaning but a designation that may require some qualification, specification, and nuancing. This is true of very many other terms and does not negate their usefulness.[58] Indeed, the flexibility of 'rape culture' and the breadth of phenomena the term encompasses are what make it appropriate for this discussion of sexual violence in the present alongside sexual violence as depicted in biblical texts. Contemporary settings are not the same as those implied by biblical rape texts but there are, nonetheless, common threads that make it fruitful to view the two side by side.

Often accompanying the perception that rape culture is too broad a term is the suggestion that 'it has gone too far', become a 'dogma', that a pendulum has swung from rape being suppressed and victims not being believed, to rape being suspected *everywhere all the time* and *all* victims being believed, even when they are making false allegations (cf. Campbell and Manning 2018: 128–29). This, as already mentioned, is very much in line with some of the 'witchhunt' responses to #MeToo. So-called moral panics, or examples of deviance amplification, do exist. They come into being when some issue is taken up and sensationalized by mass media in order to present the issue as a new and dangerous problem. In practice, however, the problem will either not be new at all – but will have captured media attention for some other reason – or may not even exist. The distorted and overblown coverage, however, will incite moral panic, often leading to increased police action and arrests. In turn, these actions and arrests will be regarded as confirmation of the growth of the problem.

A classic example of such an amplification spiral is satanic ritual abuse, allegations of which spread rapidly in the UK and beyond in the 1990s. Following a six-year investigation into these allegations, however, no evidence of such abuse, let alone of widespread satanic abuse, was ever established (Stiebert 2016: 41–42). A similarly unfounded moral panic, also with a lack of evidence, is currently erupting around allegations of predatory men feigning to be trans-women in order to gain access to women's toilets and changing rooms so as to sexually abuse women and girls. It would be wrong to claim that there have *never* been instances of false rape allegations,[59] and cases of sexual assault have a tendency to be depicted in the media in salacious and sensationalized ways.[60] But with contemporary rape culture, as demonstrated most visibly by #MeToo, the scale of abusive behaviour has been shown to be very real. Rape culture is not unfounded or a moral panic (*pace* Campbell and Manning 2018: 129). Evidence for it is abundant.

The claim of rape culture hysteria has sometimes had a displacement effect not unlike that of victim-blaming. With victim-blaming, there is sometimes more and utterly disproportionate emphasis placed on what a rape victim was wearing or drinking, rather than on the actual problem: namely, the violence and wrong committed by the perpetrator. Similarly, when there is loud noise about how vocal or hysterical those who accept the existence of rape culture or who participate in #MeToo are, there is sometimes comparably little said or done about the problem of abuse itself. As Popova (2019: 6) states, 'From random men on social media and high-profile politicians alike come questions like, "What, can't I even flirt now?," and "Do I have to sign a contract every time I have sex?" These, too, are expressions of rape culture.'

Finally, some resisters of rape culture argue that if 'culture' is the problem behind sexual violence, then this exonerates rapists. Rape, they argue, is committed because *individuals* make violent choices, not because they are shaped by a rape-supportive wider culture. To claim otherwise, they say, is to let rapists off the hook. This notion has found support from RAINN (Rape, Abuse & Incest National Network), the largest US anti-sexual violence organization, which, in its recommendations addressed to the White House, drew attention to the 'unfortunate trend towards blaming "rape culture" for the extensive problem of sexual violence on campuses' (RAINN 2014). The recommendation continues, 'it is important to not lose sight of a simple fact: Rape is caused not by cultural factors but by the conscious decisions, of a small percentage of the community, to commit a violent crime' (RAINN 2014). While rapists *are* indeed responsible and need to be held accountable for the violence they commit, it is not the case – given how many rapes are reported, let alone committed, alongside other sexualized violations of bodily autonomy – that rapes are committed by just a few 'bad apples'. Instead, the problem seems to be very much bigger. The best way to explain this is through sexual violence being sustained by structures that both reflect and promote attitudes that normalize sexualization and violence (Phillips 2017). This also explains why in some settings – for instance, where both socio-economic and gender inequalities are most pronounced – rape and other forms of sexual violence are more prevalent (e.g. Sanday 2003; Sanyal 2019: 141–63).

I argue that rape cultures are real, although they may take various and diverse forms. They have existed since antiquity and all over the world. While it is important to qualify what precisely characterizes a particular rape culture, they all share in common that sexual violence occurs and is upheld and sustained by a wider context that enables and normalizes this violence through lower-level microaggressions. Because these are part of the wider culture, microaggressions are detectable in some of the various ways culture manifests – including in the texts of the Bible and in contemporary media and popular culture – because all are products of human communities and contain many traces of what these communities believe/d and assume/d.

Another constant in both rape culture settings, ancient and modern, is that rape is experienced as traumatic by rape victims. I will not enter into any discussion as to whether some rapes are more traumatic than others, or some rape victims more resilient than others. While there are various responses to rape and a variety of ways in which individuals process rape experience, I see no compelling evidence to dissuade me that rape in the overwhelming number of cases causes profound and long-term harm to rape victims. This evidence comes from all over the world[61] and goes back as far as we have accounts by victims of rape as well as of women interpreting biblical rape stories (Schroeder 2007). Next, I will explore how rape culture is sustained in large part by rape myths.

Rape myths

The designation 'rape myth' is potentially confusing due to the two distinct meanings of the word 'myth'. On the one hand, 'myth' refers to 'a traditional story, especially one concerning the early history of a people or explaining a natural or social phenomenon, and typically involving supernatural beings or events' and, on the other, to 'a widely held but false belief or idea' (Oxford English Dictionary). There are indeed myths (in the first sense of the word) that feature rape.[62] There are numerous myths concerning Greek gods that include rape – such as the stories of Zeus seizing and raping the maidens Antiope, Callisto, Europa and Leda, and the beautiful youth Ganymede. There are also stories of Poseidon pursuing and raping Demeter and Medusa and of Hades raping Persephone. Castor and Pollux rape and afterwards marry Phoebe and Hilaeira. In Roman mythology there is the rape of Lucretia by Sextus Tarquinius, as well as the mass rape of the Sabine women by the founders of Rome. And in Christian mythology there is the story of Agnes, who consecrates her virginity to Christ and is threatened with rape in a bid to make her recant her faith.[63]

Stories from the Bible – such as the rape of Lot by his daughters or the rape of Tamar by Amnon – also qualify as myths of rape in that they are traditional stories concerning the early history of the people of Israel and involve supernatural beings or events.[64] But even though I am, in this book, discussing stories that qualify as myths and feature rape, my application of the designation 'rape myth' pertains to how this designation is most widely used: namely, to refer to false beliefs about sexual violence. Hence, I am using 'myth' in the second (falsehood) sense of the word and 'rape myths', therefore, pertains here to prejudicial or stereotyped and false beliefs about sexual assault, rapists, and victims of rape. Rape myths excuse or justify sexual aggression, provoke hostility and dismissal of rape victims, and bias public perception and criminal prosecution. In these ways rape myths are dangerous and serve to underpin and propagate rape culture.

There are very many rape myths and quite a number are attested both in the Bible and in contemporary culture, indicating their persistence, pervasiveness, and possibly, too, the Bible's influence. What follows are a few select examples of rape myths, indicating how they manifest in the Bible and in the present. Each rape myth flies in the face of facts and statistics but persists nonetheless, with damaging consequences.[65]

Victim-blaming rape myths

Some rape myths cause a significant share of the reason and blame for rape to fall on the rape victim rather than on the rapist. Explanations for rape, according to this set of myths, include that the rape victim (most often a woman) has behaved in ways that are provocative and, allegedly, rape-inciting. Such behaviour includes getting drunk, wearing revealing clothing, being promiscuous (or being regarded as promiscuous), and going to places where one should know rape happens (or where, by implication, someone respectable or more sensible would not go). Another reason (even justification) given for rape is the attractiveness of the victim, which has the subtext that a rapist cannot help themselves when sexually aroused (which constitutes another rape myth).

Evidence for the prevalence of this set of myths is very easy to find, including in contemporary media sources. In all sorts of ways the message is transmitted that victims could have prevented rape by behaving differently. Judge Lindsey Kushner was not the first judge to call on women to 'protect themselves' from rapists by staying sober (Shaw 2017). The SlutWalk, a transnational movement calling for an end to victim-blaming and rape culture, had its first rally in Toronto, Canada on 3 April 2011 in response to a Toronto police officer asserting that sexual assault could be avoided if women did not dress 'like sluts'. During a rape trial in Ireland reported on in November 2018, the defence argued, 'You have to look at the way she was dressed. She was wearing a thong with a lace front.' This gave rise to #ThisIsNotConsent, with Irish women posting pictures of their underwear. It also recalls the earlier trial of Scottish teenager Lindsay Armstrong, a rape victim who three times had to hold up the underwear she was wearing when attacked in a park near her home. Armstrong committed suicide weeks after the trial in which her attacker was found guilty (Cramb 2018). These are just a few examples, which indicate that drinking or wearing a particular kind of clothing are cited as reasons that contribute to or incite rape. Moreover, in blaming the victim, culpability is removed from the perpetrator and the criminality of the rape is downplayed, even denied.

The myth that a person's attractiveness leads to a man (in most cases) not being able to control or help himself, is also rampant. Who can forget the recording of Donald Trump, leaked during his ultimately successful campaign for the US presidency? In a tirade of braggadocio, Trump said,

> You know I'm automatically attracted to beautiful ... I just start kissing them. It's like a magnet. Just kiss. I don't even wait. And when you're a star they let you do it. You can do anything.... Grab them by the pussy. You can do anything.[66]

Here is a frank expression of abuse of power justified by victims' beauty.[67] Trump is not the only powerful man to use language of sexual coercion. Jair Bolsonaro, the current president of Brazil, told a fellow congress member, Maria do Rosário, some years before his election, 'I would never rape you because you don't deserve it' (Kaiser 2018). Similarly, Damon Wayans, defending Bill Cosby following multiple rape accusations against him, sought to ridicule the accusers' claims by judging them as 'unrapable', adding 'I look at them and go, "No, he don't want that. Get outta here!"'.[68] As Ashleigh Shackelford (2016) puts it, according to such a construction rape 'equals worthiness; a violent, misogynistic compliment we should appreciate in silence'. The success of this construction is attested by evidence that women perceived as 'plain' or 'overweight' are less likely to be believed and, consequently, less likely to report rape (Sanyal 2019: 71).

This group of rape myths is easily busted. Not only was Bill Cosby eventually convicted (though not until more than 60 women came forward to accuse him of a range of sexually violent acts, including rape) but any close, or even cursory, look at the abundant evidence shows that rape victims are not all, or even overwhelmingly, scantily dressed young women on a night out.[69] Rape victims are male, female, young, old, of any nationality, physique, skin tone, etc. – there is no 'type', physical or otherwise. Moreover, rape perpetrators are not overwhelmingly strangers spontaneously overcome by sexual desire for a woman they see in a bar or a club. Rapists are often partners or former partners, family members, acquaintances.

The association between beauty and rape (with the implication that beauty brings about and accounts for, or justifies, rape) is, however, persistent, and present also in the Bible. The sons of God rape because of human women's beauty (Genesis 6:2; cf. the retelling in 1 Enoch 7:1–2) and a number of other women who are vulnerable to rape or who are depicted as victims of rape are described as beautiful. This creates a firm association between attractiveness and rape-prone-ness and applies, for example, to Sarai (better known by her later name,

Sarah) whose beauty is praised to Pharaoh, so that he takes her for a wife[70] (Genesis 12:11–19). Mention of Bathsheba's (2 Samuel 11:2) and of Tamar's (2 Samuel 13:1) beauty also sets in motion the stories of their rape.

It is true that men, too, are described in the Bible as beautiful (see Kügler 2017) and in one instance, at least, male beauty (Genesis 39:6) exposes a man, namely Joseph, to sexual harassment and threat.[71] As in the cases of raped beautiful females – Sarai, Bathsheba, and (David's daughter) Tamar[72] – the perpetrator (though in this case, exceptionally, a woman) is a powerful social superior (Stiebert 2019: 106–07).

Beautifying oneself or behaving in other ways deemed to be sexually inciting is regularly depicted disapprovingly in the Bible. It is also a prelude to sexual violation. Hence, in Isaiah YHWH expresses displeasure at the daughters of Zion, because they 'walk with outstretched necks, glancing wantonly with their eyes, mincing along as they go, tinkling with their feet' (Isaiah 3:16, NRSV).[73] This conjures up an image of women drawing attention to themselves with their movements and ornaments; perhaps they are prancing and wearing ankle bracelets. In any case, the next verse already promises punishment: not only disfiguring scabs but also the laying bare of the women's secret parts (Isaiah 3:17). This is very clearly a sexualized kind of humiliation, such as stripping and exposing the genitals, or even rape. From here the text launches into a tirade of detail, listing all the fineries and decorations that will be taken away from the women (Isaiah 3:18–23). Instead of beauty, there will be humiliation, as she (presumably Zion) is emptied or, as the NRSV translates, ravished.

This is not a singular example. In Hosea, too, the rebuked woman is described as having something visible on her face and breasts that identifies her as promiscuous and adulterous (Hosea 2:2) (could this be make-up and a necklace?) as well as rings and jewellery (Hosea 2:13). Again, on account of this she is stripped naked and exposed (Hosea 2:3, 10).[74] In the New Testament also, women are adjured not to braid their hair or wear gold ornaments or fine clothing, because this is in conflict with inner purity (1 Peter 3:2–4). The Whore of Babylon exemplifies this clearly: she is 'clothed in purple and scarlet, and adorned with gold and jewels and pearls' (Revelation 17:4) – hence, again, beauty and beautification are associated with impurity or licentiousness. As in Isaiah and Hosea the Whore, too, is depicted as deserving of sexualized violent punishment, of being made desolate and naked, devoured and burned (Revelation 17:15).

The association between, on the one hand, feminine beauty and, on the other, sexual allure, which in turn justifies control and punishment,

is so powerful that it is even *read into* the Bible. Hence, both Eve and
Delilah are – in popular consciousness and in their long reception histo-
ries – widely depicted as beautiful, sexually alluring temptresses.[75] In
spite of this neither Eve (Genesis 2–3), nor Delilah (Judges 16) is actually ever called beautiful in the biblical text and neither emerges as a
particularly deceitful temptress either.[76] Nonetheless, both are vilified –
Eve as sinner (1 Timothy 2:13) and Delilah as quintessential *femme fatale*
(Blyth 2017). Jezebel and Potiphar's wife, too, are with little more legitimacy eroticized in their afterlives in popular culture. Jezebel has given
her name to sex workers and predatory women even though no explicit
mention is ever made of her sexuality in the Hebrew Bible.[77] Potiphar's
wife is never called beautiful or depicted as sexually enticing in Genesis
39, but is regularly depicted as alluring cougar – notably, as portrayed
by Joan Collins in the musical film *Joseph and the Amazing Technicolor
Dreamcoat* (1999). All of these biblical women – Eve, Delilah, Jezebel,
and Potiphar's wife[78] – are figures that incite anxiety or condemnation.
All are sexualized in the way they are received even though this departs
or extrapolates from the biblical text. This demonstrates first, that the
rape myth of the over-sexed and dangerous woman deserving of punishment is very powerful and sustained; and second, that biblical figures
and themes are used to promote these myths, because of their evocative
potential and cultural capital.

The notion that a victim who is either attractive or who makes
themselves attractive (through clothing or jewellery, actions or movements) invites rape has been roundly refuted. Rape has been shown
repeatedly to be motivated not by sexual desire but by a desire for
control and dominance. Consequently, 'dressing down', like other
behaviours (such as drinking less, or abstaining from flirting), does not
and cannot protect against rape. Explaining or justifying the actions of
rapists by emphasizing the looks or actions of the victim constitutes
victim-blaming and facilitates rape culture.

As demonstrated, the victim-blaming rape myth is detectable in the
Bible and persists into the present. Its established presence in the Bible
suggests that normative texts and structures of authority grounded in
these texts have validated rape-supportive attitudes. #MeToo, meanwhile, has created a momentum for challenging such attitudes – in the
Bible and elsewhere.

'Real' rape

Another set of rape myths pertains to physical force. According to this
category of myth, physical force and bodily injury are requirements of

rape. If there are no indications or evidence of concerted struggle (such as screaming, fending off, fighting, biting) and no signs of injury (such as scratches, bruises, or tearing) then whatever took place was not rape and those who later 'cry rape' may actually have wanted sex all along. Moreover, according to these myths, many people say 'no' when they mean 'yes', enjoy being overpowered, and like 'wild' or rough sex.[79]

Joy Schroeder (2007) gives numerous examples from early Church and medieval tradition, which indicate that women's desire for sex and for being sexually overpowered was presumed. Only if there was evidence of intense struggle and resistance – and even then, not in all cases – could a charge of *stuprum per vim* ('defilement by force')[80] be brought. Right up to the present day the rape kit, or collection of forensic evidence, including evidence of injury to the rape victim's body (such as bruising) and evidence of resistance (e.g. traces of the perpetrator's DNA under the victim's fingernails), can be instrumental in determining whether a rape case goes to court and has a good chance of conviction.

The myth persists that rape is rape *only* if the victim screams, struggles, and keeps on fighting. It is enmeshed with related myths that women will routinely resist and delay sex when really they want it. This, in turn, stems from widespread cultural expectations and scripts that determine that a man should 'chase' the woman in whom he is sexually interested and that women should not be 'too easy', should feign disinterest and keep a man waiting before, eventually, with apparent reluctance, succumbing. The difficulties of this are clear. It imparts that 'no' should not be understood as 'no' but as 'yes please', and that men's aggressive and pushy behaviour is sometimes positively encouraged.

Moreover, right up to the present, cases can hinge on the suggestion that what may appear to be violent rape is actually consensual 'wild' sex – the subtext being that (many) women 'like it rough'[81] (Kale 2016; American Media Inc. 2018; BBC 2018; Duff 2018).[82] Underpinned by such rape myths, rape complainants[83] are questioned and doubted when sex is rough, even brutal. But rape complainants are also questioned and doubted when they are *not* expressive. If women fight, they are being sexually 'wild'; if they do not, they are interpreted to be compliant and complicit; often, in neither case is an allegation of rape accepted.

There are good reasons why a rape victim might *not* scream or resist when subjected to assault – most obvious among them being terror. Many victims report 'freezing' or a feeling of dissociation from their bodies both during and for some time after rape. And yet, not screaming or resisting, is still sometimes equated with consent and 'not rape'.

A particularly horrific example of this is a recent case in northern Spain, named after the accused men's WhatsApp group, *la manada*, Spanish for 'the wolf pack'. The verdict in respect of the five men accused of gang-raping an 18-year-old woman was that they were guilty of sexual abuse rather than the more severe offence of rape. This is because, in Spanish law, 'only sex that involves violence or intimidation can constitute rape' and the woman was deemed to have adopted 'an attitude of submission and subjugation' – moreover, according to one judge, 'in an atmosphere of fun and revelry' (Rosell 2018). Some 96 seconds of footage from the men's phones shows the woman immobile and with her eyes closed during the attack. The defence proposed such a lack of active and physical resistance was proof of consent. The prosecution argued against this, claiming that the victim had been too frightened to move. Victoria Rosell (2018), criminal court judge with 20 years' experience, describes the footage as 'of a young woman cornered and unable to react, literally paralysed, surrounded by five men, all older and stronger than her, in a narrow lobby with only one exit'. It seems utterly superfluous to have to justify why the woman was terrified and did not resist and it is cruel to suggest consent. As prosecutor Elena Sarasate put it with unsparing bluntness,

> [t]he defendants want us to believe that on that night they met an 18-year-old girl, living a normal life, who – after 20 minutes of conversation with people she didn't know – agreed to group sex involving every type of penetration, sometimes simultaneously, without using a condom.
>
> (Jones 2018)

The verdict led to large protests, directed not only at this case but at 'a system in which chauvinism is structural and institutional' (Rosell 2018) – in other words, at rape culture.[84]

Again, both the rape myths that women are sexually rampant and therefore invite sexual violence and that rape only 'counts' if a woman has screamed and resisted are present in the Bible. I have already, just above, discussed the former with reference to the books of both Hosea and Revelation. Added to this is the rape of Jerusalem in Jeremiah 13, cast in the familiar prophetic woman metaphor. Again, the woman is charged with being sexually rampant: she is accused of adulteries and shameless prostitution, which are given as the justification for rape (Jeremiah 13:26–27). Similarly, feminized Jerusalem in the book of Ezekiel 'play[s] the whore' and lavishes '[her] whorings on any passer-by' (Ezekiel 16:15–16, NRSV), in every square and at the head of every street (Ezekiel 16:24–25), even paying her lovers rather than receiving payment, which is intended to portray her as worse and more depraved than a sex worker[85] (Ezekiel 16:33–34). This sexual excess is met – by implication legitimately – with God-her-husband's fury and jealousy (Ezekiel 16:42).[86]

That rape is only considered 'real' rape if a man seizes a woman and she screams and resists is also evident in the Bible. This is most clear in the distinction between the two scenarios in Deuteronomy 22:23–27. As already mentioned (p. 31), the first concerns a virgin betrothed to be married. In this case, if a man 'meets her in the town and lies with her', both are to be stoned to death: the man, because he violated another man's wife and the woman, 'because she did not cry for help in the town' (Deuteronomy 22:24). The man is clearly the active agent in this scenario: he is the subject of the verbs 'meet', 'lies with', and 'violates'. The woman is clearly passive: she is met, slept with and violated. She is, nonetheless, held to be co-responsible, even complicit, because she was not heard to cry out in a (presumably) populated place. The description of the scenario indirectly acknowledges the woman's vulnerability: she is sexually inexperienced (a virgin) and a man other than the one to whom she is betrothed targets her. But she is not exonerated from blame and no allowance is made for her not crying out for help. Factors such as coercion, intimidation, threat, the rapist smothering her cries, or terror silencing her – none of these are cited as concessions.

In the second scenario the man meets a betrothed woman in the open country. This time if he seizes her and lies with her, then only the man is to be killed. The woman is not deemed to have done anything punishable by death, 'because she may have cried for help, but there was no one to rescue her' (Deuteronomy 22:27). In this scenario the woman is not co-responsible and what has befallen her appears to be equivalent with *stuprum per vim*, 'defilement by force'. Only in the second scenario is presence of the perpetrator's force and absence of the victim's consent accepted – in the first scenario, the latter, or both, are denied.

Other pronouncements in the proximity of these two scenarios make it clear that adultery – rather than rape – is envisaged as the 'real' crime (Deuteronomy 22:22). Hence, if a man 'meets' a virgin who is *not* betrothed, and he seizes her and lies with her, then, if they are discovered, the man must pay the woman's father and take her as a wife without possibility of divorce (Deuteronomy 22:28–29). The verb 'seize' suggests force (cf. Numbers 5:13)[87] and what can be inferred here is that rape is a way to marriage and marriage a way of 'fixing' damage caused by rape.[88] While the rapist *is* punished, the punishment pales next to that for adultery. The possibility, even probability, that the woman would feel horror at marrying her rapist receives no considera-tion here or elsewhere in the Bible. Instead, rape is depicted as little more than sex, with no appreciation of the violence and trauma attending rape.

It should also be added that in terms of a face-value reading of the biblical text, the death penalty is repeatedly given as punishment for unlawful sex, with no opt-out clause for rape. This applies to both male and female possible victims of rape. In cases of adultery, where a man lies with the wife of another man, both are to be executed. While the man's sexual initiative is (as elsewhere) presumed in such a sexual encounter and with no clarity as to whether the woman was or was not forced, the death penalty applies to both (Deuteronomy 22:22; Leviti-cus 20:10). A woman found not to have been a virgin prior to marriage is also to be executed by stoning – on account of having '[prostituted] herself in her father's house' (Deuteronomy 22:21).[89] Likewise, if a man has sex with a male,[90] both are to be put to death (Leviticus 20:13). The possibility of rape is not mentioned as a mitigating circumstance in either case.

The rape myth of what constitutes 'real' rape is represented in the Bible and in the present. There are certainly pronounced distinctions between the disparate rape cultures – hence, the biblical 'solution' that an unbetrothed woman who is raped should marry her rapist is *not* pro-posed in Western democratic settings, nor is adultery accorded any-where near the horror and condemnation with which it is depicted in the Bible. But the myth that physical violence is required for something to 'count' as rape persists, as does the myth that rape is 'just' sex, or wild sex, part of normal heterosexual dynamics, rather than a distressing act of violence against the bodily autonomy of the victim.

Also related to the myth about 'real' rape is the rape myth that women (in most cases) regularly make false allegations about rape. The reasons given for such false allegations are usually that women either regret having sex, or want to get 'even' with a man (maybe because they did not enjoy sex or because the man otherwise disappointed or later rejected them), or that they want attention. In the wake of #MeToo, the accusation that women are revising the past and 'jumping on the bandwagon' is also becoming apparent. There are numerous suggestions, for instance, that actresses joining #MeToo were happy in times past to advance their careers by having sex with influential men in the film industry, only later to 'cry rape' when this was, in a new setting, expedient in terms of getting attention and publicity. Such has been claimed not only by Weinstein's lawyer Benjamin Brafman (Pavia

2018)[91] but also by Germaine Greer (Kaplan 2018).[92] The effect of such claims is to downplay, first, the seriousness and harmfulness of sexual assault; second, the role and responsibility of often very powerful men; and third, the self-evident fact (given the abundance of #MeToo disclosures) that harassment and rape have occurred with alarming frequency and impunity over a long period of time.[93]

Are there examples of women who have made false allegations of rape? Yes, there are. Do such allegations harm innocently accused persons? Absolutely.[94] The story of Jemma Beale, infamous for making multiple false rape accusations, one of which led to the wrongful imprisonment of a man, received intense publicity in England and Beale became a target of the kind of hatefulness and vitriol usually reserved for child killers. There is no dispute about Beale having acted despicably – but the rarity of cases of false allegation needs to be kept in mind – especially alongside the much more enormous number of rape cases that are not reported, not brought before the court, or which do not transpire in guilty verdicts even where evidence is quite strong.[95]

Rape perpetrators

I have already looked at the rape myth that rape victims invite or bring about their attack – because of their conduct, or because they are attractive. As discussed, there is no 'type' when it comes to rape victims. This also applies to rape perpetrators. And yet, according to other deeply entrenched rape myths, rapists also conform to 'type' and are expected, for example, to be strangers, lurking behind bushes or in dark alleys. Instead, rather more often, rapists are acquaintances of their victims, or former or current intimate partners. Still, the influence of the 'stranger danger' myth contributes to victims who report persons they know and whom they may have dated as rapists, being disbelieved. It has also led, in readings of the Bible, to not recognizing the rape of Hagar, for instance, as rape (Genesis 16:3–4), presumably because she was part of Abram's household and Abram, therefore, no stranger.

Another aspect of the 'type' rape myth purports that men of certain 'races' or ethnicities are more likely to be rapists. The idea of 'race' has been shown to have no genetic or other scientific basis. But if we either take 'race' to refer to physical and genetically determined characteristics, such as colouration of skin, hair, and eyes, or if we opt for 'ethnicity', which refers to cultural markers, including nationality, regional and religious customs, and language, the idea that some kinds of men (e.g. Black men, Jewish men, Mexican men, migrant men) are more prone to raping, still does not stand up to scrutiny.

Racialization and its construction of some groups as 'other' on the basis of ethnic origin or of skin colouration has a long and deep history of significantly contributing to both racism and rape culture. In the USA, for example, rape has been prominently conceptualized as a crime predominantly perpetrated by Black men against white women[96] – in no small part in order deliberately to reframe and to erase a history of white men raping Black and indigenous women who, to this day, continue to experience much higher rates of sexual violence than white women (Crenshaw 1991; Edwards 2018; Popova 2019: 26).

Such rape myths resonate well beyond the USA, however. As Sanyal (2019: 90–96) has expounded, the image of men of 'Arabic and North African appearance' has become inseparably linked with sexual threats to white women in Germany, just as 'Asian men' have become particularly associated with grooming and raping vulnerable white girls in the UK. In neither context, however, is there any statistical support either for minority ethnic men showing an increased propensity to rape, or for inter-ethnic rape being a more widely committed crime than intra-ethnic rape.

Again, the Bible is not blameless in terms of perpetuating sexualized ethnic stereotypes. These pertain to both men and women. First, some of its texts help to convey not only that women *generally* are prone to sexual depravity (thereby inviting or justifying sexually violent punishment) but also that 'other' or 'foreign' women are *particularly* sexually depraved (and therefore, by implication, even more deserving of violent treatment). While there are discrepancies,[97] the dominant ideology is that foreign women are dangerous and justly maligned. The seductive adulteress of Proverbs is 'strange' and 'foreign' (Proverbs 7:5). Strong Samson is brought down in part by his attraction to foreign (Philistine) women (Judges 14), as is wise King Solomon (1 Kings 11:1–10; Nehemiah 13:26). Moabite women jeopardize the Israelites in the wilderness (Numbers 25) and women of the land (such as Canaanites and Moabites) pollute the 'holy seed' (Ezra 9:1–2).

Foreign men are likewise associated with sexual deviance as well as with rape in the Hebrew Bible. It is in Egypt that feminized Samaria and Jerusalem have their breasts and nipples groped (Ezekiel 23:3, 8, 21) by men with grotesque genitals and emissions (Ezekiel 23:20); it is Assyrians who 'uncover … nakedness' (Ezekiel 23:10), an expression that elsewhere implies prohibited sexual acts, such as incest (Leviticus 18:6)[98] and sex with a menstruant (Leviticus 18:19); and it is Babylonian lovers who disgust even the depraved Oholibah (Ezekiel 23:17). Egyptian Pharaoh rapes Sarai (Genesis 12:19; cf. the threat posed to Israelite women by Abimelech of Gerar in Genesis 20 and 26:6–11) and Hivite Shechem rapes Dinah (Genesis 34:2).

There are Israelite rapists, too: it is when the Levite eschews sojourning in Jebusite territory to avoid 'a city of foreigners, who do not belong to the people of Israel' (Judges 19:12) that his wife is gang-raped in the Israelite territory of Benjamin. Amnon, the royal firstborn, and King David himself are rapists (2 Samuel 11–13). Indeed, the more prominent message is that sex with a foreigner is the problem – a much greater problem than rape by a fellow Israelite. The latter can be resolved[99] – as long as adultery has not been committed. But where a foreigner is concerned, even marriage cannot make amends. Hence, Jacob's sons refer to Shechem's request for marriage as a disgrace, on account of his being uncircumcised (Genesis 34:14) and go on to avenge what they consider the defilement of their sister (Genesis 34:5, 13) even after the Hivites undergo circumcision. Likewise, the marriage of Israelite Zimri to Cozbi, a Midianite woman, is depicted as abhorrent: Phinehas the priest is praised for his zeal and for turning back divine anger when he kills the couple (Numbers 25:6–16).

The Bible contains ideologies that render non-Israelites as 'other' and suspect, including in sexual terms. This plays a part in perpetuating rape myths that construct 'other' (such as Black) women as rapable and 'other' (such as Black) men as rapists. In multiple ways, therefore, the contexts reflected in and by biblical texts are rape cultures. Rape cultures of the past and the present are different (as is to be expected) but both are sustained in significant ways by rape myths. Some rape myths firmly entrenched in the present do have affinity with attitudes inculcated in the Bible.

Notes

1 To give an example, Melanie Phillips (2018), reporting on her participation in a debate on the motion 'That MeToo has gone too far' (alongside Germaine Greer and against Helena Kennedy and Sophie Walker), writes that #MeToo demonizes men in general and exhibits 'disproportionality, complicity and hypocrisy' alongside 'vanity, narcissism and arrogance'. For her, #MeToo is mostly about 'injustice, gender-hate and sub-Marxist claptrap … a betrayal of the cause of women everywhere' (Phillips 2018). I disagree with Phillips and concur instead with Michelle Goldberg that what is vastly exaggerated is the idea of #MeToo going too far or of striking men down at random, or unfairly. As Goldberg adds, it *is* unusual that some powerful men have suffered consequences and lost their jobs: 'that's where the cultural panic comes from; it's panic about the end of male impunity' (Griffiths 2018: 17). On women's backlash to feminism, of which Phillips is representative, see Banet-Weiser (2015).

2 For a compelling study contrasting the considerable discrepancies between newspaper reports of certain kinds of sexual violence (in this case father–daughter incest) and independent evidence of the actual incidence of the same crime, alongside reasons for this discrepancy, see Sacco (2009).

3 Jameson (1981) argues that *all* texts – ancient and modern – owe their inception to the existence and repression (be it conscious or not) of socio-political conflict. Clines (2009 [1995]: 94–121) makes this case for biblical texts using the example of Song of Songs and demonstrating affinities in response to this book between ancient and modern readers.

4 Whether #MeToo actually helps (all) those who disclose, or (all/any of) those affected by sexual violence who do not disclose but follow the movement is harder to establish (See Casewell 2017; Mendes *et al.* 2019: 5, 188).

5 I will use 2 Samuel 13 as my primary example text from the Bible, because it is the narrative most easily identified as a rape text, given that the rapist's physical force and the rape victim's absence of consent are explicitly stated.

6 I am in agreement with Clines (2009 [1995]: 13) that theology is a sub-set of ideology.

7 'YHWH' is a transliteration of the four Hebrew letters known as 'the Tetragrammaton' (Greek for 'the four letters'), which signify the divine name. In English bibles this is often rendered 'the LORD' in capital letters.

8 Outside of the biblical text, however, there is no independent verification for their existence, with the possible exception of David who is named in a few extra-biblical inscriptions. Notable among these inscriptions is the Tel Dan stele, which refers to the 'house of David', likely to be a reference to the dynasty founded by King David. The inscription is dated to 870–750 BCE: that is, well after what has been proposed by biblical scholars as the lifetime of David. David's reign tends to be dated to *c.*1000 BCE. Consequently, the stele would seem to indicate David's fame and posterity.

9 Cf. Blyth (2010: 11) who stresses the same of Dinah.

10 By tearing of the very robe that distinguishes her as a royal virgin daughter (2 Samuel 13:18–19), Tamar re-enacts the violence that was done to her: the tearing of her hymen. Elsewhere agency is denied but what *is done to* women's bodies is nonetheless expressive: hence, Dinah is taken by her brothers, harking back to Shechem taking her (Genesis 34:2, 26) and the Levite's wife's gesture, of her hands on the threshold of the house from which she was cast out to the rapists, is performative of helpless despair (Judges 19:27). Also, the sharing of her body parts among men of Israel conjures up again the gang-rape in Gibeah (Judges 19:27, 29).

11 'Interests' refers to ideological investments and agendas. As Clines (2009: 23–25) expounds, such are held by both writers and readers of texts.

12 See above and Introduction, Note 24.

13 Schroeder's fascinating study of early Church to Reformation Christian interpretations of biblical rape texts points out, furthermore, that while 'an extraordinary number of commentators chose to reflect upon Genesis 34', there is nonetheless 'nearly complete absence of women's commentary on the passage' (Schroeder 2007: 51). What *is* there, however, while isolated and rare, often does represent 'a spirited defense of women' (Schroeder 2007: 51). Schroeder (2007: 53–54) refers to Christine de Pizan (1363–*c.*1431) and Arcangela Tarabotti (1604–54) who both articulate the horrors of rape for women. It is not that women did not suffer rape or have strong views on the subject but that women are barely represented in what has been transmitted and preserved. With the story of the gang-rape of the Levite's wife (Judges 19) there are no extant female discussions at all prior to the eighteenth and nineteenth centuries (Schroeder 2007: 152).

14 See Mendes *et al.* (2019: 2–5) for this phrase, as well as on how traditionally unempowered groups, such as teenage schoolgirls, have used digital technologies for large-scale and effective protest movements.

15 'The West' is used as shorthand here to refer to the non-Communist states of Europe, alongside North America and Australia and New Zealand. All of these geographical regions are historically associated with economic and social power, privilege, and entitlement. Hall cautions that while '[w]e have to use short-hand generalizations, like "West" and "western", … we need to remember that they represent very complex ideas and have no simple or single meaning' (Hall 1992: 276–77). He also explains that 'the West' is not a geographical designation so much as a concept pertaining to 'a society that is developed, industrialized, urbanized, capitalist, secular, and modern' (Hall 1992: 276–77).

16 According to the Thomson Reuters Foundation poll on 'Most Dangerous Countries for Women' of 2018, which includes the criterion of 'sexual violence', the ten worst countries were (in order): India, Afghanistan, Syria, Somalia, Saudi Arabia, Pakistan, Democratic Republic of Congo, Yemen, Nigeria, and the USA. The Armed Conflict Location and Event Data project of 2019, meanwhile, reported an increase in sexual violence, especially against women and girls, with the Democratic Republic of Congo designated most violent, followed by India, South Sudan, Burundi, Mozambique, and Zimbabwe (Austin 2019). With the exception of the USA, members of the other countries are proportionally severely underrepresented in #MeToo. R. S. Sugirtharajah (2008) makes a similar point regarding under-representation of Two-Thirds world interpretation in biblical studies in his edited volume gloomily and aptly entitled *Still at the Margins: Biblical Scholarship Fifteen Years after the Voices from the Margin*.

17 A recent report based on research for the UK Trades Union Congress speaks of a 'hidden epidemic' and reports the very high incidence of sexual harassment in the workplace, with Black Minority Ethnic women, LGBT persons, and persons with disabilities particularly vulnerable (Perraudin 2019; cf. numerous contributions in Lombard 2018). All of these groups are far less visible in #MeToo than white, straight women (see Rodriguez 2018).

18 As Colgan and Blyth (2018: 202) point out, in the university classroom, too, biblical texts depicting gender violence come as a surprise for both Christian and non-Christian students alike.

19 A report on the 2019 Cannes film festival characterizes the impact of #MeToo in ambivalent terms (Bakare 2019). The report describes the 'shockwaves' sent through the film industry when, at the 2018 Cannes awards ceremony, actor and director Asia Argento announced that she was raped at Cannes in 1997 by Harvey Weinstein. One year on, there is a hotline for those wanting to report sexual aggressors and there are efforts to offer 'services aimed at making the festival more attractive to families' – but there are also charges of 'unworkable gimmickry' and of things being 'business as usual'.

20 Carroll (1997 [1991]: 9–10) describes the Bible as 'an essentially alien work (or congeries of alien books)' and, memorably, writes, 'If reading the Bible does *not* raise profound problems for you as a modern reader, then check with your doctor and enquire about the symptoms of brain-death' (Carroll 1997 [1991]: 2).

21 See also Chapter 1, Note 60.
22 In her book *Fragmented Women*, Exum (2015 [1993]) provides a careful analysis of the subtle ways in which narrative methods reflect and propel violence against both women and female literary characters. Weems (1995: 1),
meanwhile, opens her monograph *Battered Love*, which is centred on sexual
violence in prophetic metaphor, with the chilling question, 'What in the
image of a naked, mangled female body grips the religious imagination?'.
Both writers move from analysis of violent biblical texts to the impact of
these texts on present-day readers and communities.
23 Scholz (2018: 187–90) gives a succinct summary of key monographs that
have appeared on this topic in the first decade of the twenty-first century.
The majority of these are feminist texts. Added to this can be the very many
journal articles and the widespread emergence of biblical studies modules
focused on gender, sexuality, and/or violence. For some critical reflection
on this, see Graybill (No date), 'Focus On Teaching about Sexual Violence
in the Hebrew Bible'.
24 For a host of examples, see The Shiloh Project as well as the #SheToo
podcast series of the Bible Society.
25 An activist handbook on rape culture from 2005 contains contributions on
the church and rape in marriage (Adams 2005), as well as on sexual abuse
by clergy and religious leaders (Fortune 2005). The other two volumes
edited by Blyth *et al.* (2018) focus on interdisciplinary and on Christian perspectives and also provide a host of examples of how rape culture and religious communities intersect. Hashtags from other religious communities are
#TempleToo and #MosqueToo, for Hindu and Muslim victims of sexual
abuse, respectively.
26 For a vociferous challenge to the notion that biblical literacy is in decline,
see the contributions in Edwards (2015).
27 Brown and Carasso (2013) describe the marketization and commercializa-
tion of higher education in England as part of a growing worldwide trend.
They argue, however, that in England, marketization has possibly pro-
ceeded furthest. The impetus for this ongoing process was, they argue, the
introduction of full cost fees for international students in 1980.
28 At the majority of universities, including where I teach, this scrutiny is
focused on biblical texts in modern translation.
29 The University and College Union (UCU) began strike actions in 64
universities on 22 February 2018, as part of industrial action on account of
proposed changes to the Universities Superannuation Scheme. This was to
become the longest ever strike in UK higher education history to date. An
estimated 42,000 staff participated in the strike. While 126,000 students
signed petitions calling for fee refunds, students also occupied campus build-
ings in support of striking staff in more than a dozen universities.
30 Occupy is short for 'Occupy Wall Street'. This movement emerged in 2011
in New York City's financial district to protest against economic inequality.
It quickly moved beyond New York. Alongside occupation and other
forms of civil disobedience, such as picketing and demonstrations, the
movement also practised internet activism.
31 This movement, abbreviated as XR, is a non-violent resistance movement
protesting against climate breakdown and the mass extinctions of species
and biodiversity loss. It was formed in late October 2018.

32 For example, on Occupy and outspoken and Bible-founded support from the Vatican, see Squires (2011). On XR and religious forms of protest, see Skrimshire (2019), who stresses that religious rituals are 'not enacted as a reflective "aside" from the main [XR] protests but acts of protest in themselves'.

33 Among the 'chestnuts' here is 2 Samuel 24:1 compared with 1 Chronicles 21:1. In the first passage YHWH incites David to take a census but in the retelling it is Satan who does so. Another example is a comparison of the slavery laws in Exodus 21:1–6, Leviticus 25:39–46, and Deuteronomy 15:12–18. Again, the three are not aligned.

34 Given how prominently the biblical text has been privileged with authority, examples of prooftexting are commonplace. Hence, to give just one example, Genesis 1:27–28 is widely applied to justify monogamous marriage between one man and one woman (and to vilify same-sex marriage) – even though the verses say nothing about marriage.

35 For a summary of this, see Stone (2018). I am grateful to Brandon Hurlbert for alerting me to this information. Similarly, Donald Trump has been exonerated both for his boasts of sexual assault and his affair with Stormy Daniels through comparison with biblical King David, 'a man after God's own heart' (Coaston 2018).

36 Brownmiller and her ideas are sometimes labelled as radical feminist (e.g. Phillips 2017: 7). Feminism is, of course, poly-vocal, and includes among other subsets, anarchist, Black and womanist, French, Eco- and liberal feminisms. Radical feminism aims at a comprehensive reordering of patriarchal society so as to eliminate male supremacy in all social and economic contexts towards the realization of gender equality. Brownmiller, expressing herself in binary terms, conceives of men as oppressors and women as oppressed, with rape as a weapon of the patriarchy. The most famous sentence of her book argues that rape 'is nothing more or less than a conscious process of intimidation by which *all* men keep *all* women in a state of fear' (Brownmiller 1975: 15).

37 See Note 18 above.

38 As has been and will be discussed, some feminists (e.g. Greer, Sanyal) have criticized what they characterize as a tendency towards victim feminism. Sanyal (2019: 61–84), for instance, resists the idea that there is only one 'real' response to rape (e.g. collapsing and being damaged and traumatized ever after). The sociologists Campbell and Manning (2018: 128–29) characterize rape culture as a manifestation of victimhood culture.

39 This short documentary includes contributions from rapists, rape victims, and rape crisis workers, alongside an interview with feminist, academic, and theologian Mary Daly and excerpts from mass media that show how rape is normalized, even romanticized.

40 Harding (2015: 2) draws attention to this 'bold, shocking choice of words' but determines it is 'not much of an exaggeration'.

41 Sanyal has much to say about what she considers the mis-gendering of rape. She points not only to the rather high incidence of male–male rape (e.g. Sanyal 2019: 131–32) but to men 'being made to penetrate' by women (Sanyal 2019: 125). She states, 'this in no way suggests that men are the "real" victims. But it does suggest that we should reconsider how we speak about rape and gender, and stop unthinkingly assuming, it is always something only men do to women' (Sanyal 2019: 132).

42 See Note 14 above.
43 For a series of examples of violence targeting women from many different parts of the world, see Lloyd-Roberts and Morris (2016). For a study of female perpetrators that discusses sexual violence in gendered terms and acknowledges females as most victimized, see Sjoberg (2016).
44 The title of Phillips' book alludes to the controversial song and album *Blurred Lines* by Robin Thicke and Pharrell Williams, which was released in 2013. The lyrics and music video were criticized for being misogynistic and for promoting a culture of date rape. The song was banned in the UK from some institutions and university student unions.
45 See Crown Prosecution Service (2017).
46 See Introduction, Notes 10 and 12.
47 The Bible indeed seems to imply that rape of a man is worse than rape of a woman. Hence, in both Genesis 19 and Judges 19 rape of a man is deemed abhorrent and females, including virgin daughters, are offered up for rape instead (cf. Stone 1996).
48 See also Popova (2019: 30–31) who argues similarly that any ' "tiering" of sexual offenses, with penetrative rape at the "top," creates a structure that privileges some sexual acts over others, implying that some sexual acts "count" more than others'.
49 Whoopi Goldberg, notoriously, stated that Roman Polanski was not guilty of what she termed 'rape-rape' but presumably of some 'lesser' rape, again implying rape ranking (Kennedy 2009). In not dissimilar fashion, Barbra Streisand mitigated Michael Jackson's abuse of Wade Robson and James Safechuck when both were children, even though she believed them 'absolutely'. Streisand, who later apologized for her words, said in an interview with *The Times*, 'You can say "molested", but those children, … they were thrilled to be [at Jackson's Neverland ranch]. They both married and they both have children, so it didn't kill them' (Lartey 2019). Sexual abuse, even of children, is downplayed – be it on account of the celebrity status of the (admired?) perpetrator, or on the (unfounded) assessment that the victim is 'alright', or both. The comments by both Goldberg and Streisand imply that rape or molestation is not always 'that bad'.
50 Sanyal (2019: 168) reports on studies with refugees of ethnic cleansing. These refugees talked about the experience of rape in ways very different from rape victims in many clinical studies conducted in Western countries. The refugees depicted their rape in desexualized terms, on a par with other experiences of brutality, and in no uncertain terms as to the wrongfulness of what had befallen them. They did not report feelings of shame.
51 At the time of writing the death of Noa Pothoven was reported. Pothoven refused to eat or drink and died at the age of 17 at her parents' home in the Netherlands, after a prolonged period of depression and anorexia following sexual molestation at the age of 11 and rape at the age of 14 (Henley 2019). See also the quotation by Gay (p. 18).
52 Sanyal discusses a number of cases, including those of Samantha Geimer (Sanyal 2019: 78–83) and Natascha Kampusch (Sanyal 2019: 66–68). Geimer was raped as a child by Roman Polanski and described relentless media intrusion as constantly re-traumatizing and ultimately more harmful than her experience of rape. Kampusch, meanwhile, wanted to leave her traumatic experiences behind her and move on with her life. Both met with

persistent intrusion in their lives and with accusations of being in denial. Another case Sanyal (2019: 147–53) discusses is of Thordis Elva and Tom Stranger. Stranger raped Elva when both were teenagers. Years later, seeking a form of restorative justice, Elva prompted Stranger to meet her on neutral ground and to confront the rape together. They went on to co-author a book, *South of Forgiveness*. Some events promoting this book had to be cancelled on account of public criticism that the book constituted a rape apology or that promotional events gave a public platform to a self-confessed rapist. All of these cases show, first, that rape is processed differently by different individuals and, second, (unsurprisingly) that media and members of the public can be insensitive and intrusive. But all cases confirm that rape is traumatic and neither Sanyal nor Veselka deny this.

53 There are patterns and tendencies, but many first responders report that victims of rape can feel numb and act undemonstratively, or, alternatively, can feel frightened and act in emotionally heightened ways. Again, there is no script.

54 For example, Rape Crisis England & Wales state on their website, 'When we work with survivors, we are led by them, encourage them to name and frame their own experiences, and use the language they find most meaningful and reflexive of what they've been through' (https://rapecrisis.org.uk/get-informed/about-sexual-violence/myths-vs-realities/).

55 In both the biblical text and some modern examples, victim responses to rape may sometimes seem counter-intuitive, discomforting, or as departing from expectations. This, in turn, can transpire in suppression of that which is deemed anomalous. Graybill (forthcoming) is correct that Tamar's desire to marry her rapist-brother is difficult to accommodate in most consent discourses. In Graybill's assessment, Tamar's desire is '*fuzzy/messy/icky*', which, for her, explains why commentators focus on Tamar's rape and on 'mourning with/for Tamar' but not on why she wants to marry Amnon. To give two similarly disconcerting examples from actual (not literary) rape victims: first, Jill Saward, a victim of rape in a vicious attack at the vicarage of St. Mary's in Ealing in 1986, in her book *Rape: My Story*, discloses her disappointment that she did not get pregnant following the rape (Sanyal 2019: 64). Second, there are reports of women rescued from Boko Haram who are returning to their captors who had in some cases raped them – because the wider repercussions of any set of circumstances can be acutely complicated and evoke a range of responses (Nwaubani 2018). Again, however, neither the biblical nor the autobiographical or news report account takes away from the dreadfulness of rape. Each instead testifies that there is no formula or script for the effects of rape.

56 For a fuller discussion of rape culture denial and some of its shades of dissent, see Stiebert 2017 and 2018.

57 Occasionally, a society, such as the Minangkabau of West Sumatra, is singled out as not manifesting sexual violence (Sanday 2003). Even in societies where violence is rare, there tend to be markers of hierarchy, including gendered hierarchy. Possibly, lower-tier microaggressions are present here too.

58 In my investigation of incest in the Hebrew Bible (Stiebert 2016) it became clear very quickly that while incest is regarded as a universal human phenomenon, what constitutes (illegal) incest, as opposed to (legal) close-kin marriage is carefully and variously culturally prescribed. Marriage, too, with

reference to the Bible, pertains to a range of practices and includes levirate marriage, polygyny, monogamy, and rape marriage among others. Like 'incest' and 'marriage', 'rape culture' sometimes requires delineation. It is nevertheless a useful and meaningful designation.

59 The case of Jemma Beale, jailed for ten years in August 2017 for making several false allegations of rape, was very prominent in the UK media (Stiebert 2019: 108–09).

60 Sanyal (2019: 46–48) discusses several such cases, including that of weatherman Jörg Kachelmann and his ex-girlfriend Claudia D., 'Germany's most prolific rape case of the last decade'. The coverage of Harvey Weinstein's abuses has also sometimes descended into lurid and gross details. While these details may well be true, media coverage has sometimes served to amplify the grotesque at the expense of focusing on the harm Weinstein's abuses have wrought.

61 There is much evidence for this in many of the sources consulted for this volume. Most compelling, perhaps, is the investigation by the Economist Intelligence Unit (2019).

62 On the archaic use of 'rape' as in the title 'The Rape of Helen', referring to a story that is part of a larger mythology cycle, see p. 2.

63 In some versions of the story of Saint Agnes any man who attempted to rape her was instantly struck blind. The prefect's son was struck dead – but revived after Agnes prayed for him. There are other brutal accounts of female saints venerated for their persistence in fending off sexual assault (see Schroeder 2007: 57–99) – such as St. Maria Goretti, St. Agatha, and St. Solange.

64 The story of Lot and his daughters (Genesis 19) qualifies as myth: it is preceded by the divine destruction of Sodom and Gomorrah and tells of the origins of the peoples of Moab and Ammon. The rape of Tamar, as discussed above (p. 46), is part of the divinely foretold outworkings of her father David's sin.

65 For a fuller list of common rape myths alongside realities, with statistics, see Rape Crisis England & Wales (No date).

66 The transcript of the videotape recorded prior to Trump's appearance in an episode of a US television soap opera is widely available. First revealed by the *Washington Post*, it is published also by the *New York Times* and the BBC.

67 Since, and in a similar vein, Trump dismissed E. Jean Carroll's accusation of sexual assault with 'she's not my type'. Carroll is the sixteenth woman to accuse Trump of sexual misconduct (Zurcher 2019).

68 This brings in another rape myth, namely, that women often accuse men falsely of rape – either because they regret sex, or because they want revenge or attention. In reality, malicious false rape allegations are rare. The Bible contains the story of Potiphar's wife (Genesis 39) who, when her attempt at forcing Joseph to have sex with her fails, seizes his garment and uses this as proof to support the lie that Joseph attempted to rape her. I discuss this story alongside false rape allegation, and the rape myth of false rape allegation being commonplace and ruining many innocent men's lives, elsewhere (Stiebert 2019). In the scenario described in Deuteronomy 22:25–27, the impression is given that the word of the woman raped in the open country is believed. This can lead to the execution of the rapist, while

the woman is spared. In contrast to Genesis 39, this suggests that women may have been believed, or not regularly suspected of fabricating rape lies.

69 One visually striking record of this was the poignant exhibition of clothing worn by rape survivors at the time of their rape. The clothing was on display at the Centre Communautaire Maritime in Brussels and included evening dresses but also a child's T-shirt bearing a cartoon, a school uniform, and a wide array of other unexceptional outfits (Kennelly and Madi 2018).

70 The expression 'to take for a wife' seems to refer less to a ceremony (such as a wedding or other marriage ritual) and more to taking for sex (cf. Genesis 16:3, of Sarai giving Hagar to Abram).

71 There is no need or reason to assume that Lot's angel-guests are 'heavenly handsome' men towards whom the men of Sodom feel overwhelming erotic attraction. Their attractiveness or otherwise receives no mention. The men of Sodom are, conceivably, motivated not by lust but by a desire to demonstrate their dominance and power. This would be entirely typical of rape motivation (Genesis 19:1–5).

72 These are a few of the clearest examples. The list can be extended to include also the captive woman (Deuteronomy 21:11–14) and Esther (Esther 2:2–4, 7, 12–17).

73 Cf. also the adulteress of Proverbs 6–7 who is likened to a 'prostitute' (7:10, NRSV) and who seduces with enticing eyelashes (6:25).

74 Another, lengthy example is feminized Jerusalem in Ezekiel 16. She, too, is beautiful and richly ornamented, which leads on to her whorings and adulteries, followed by violent punishment (Ezekiel 16:10–43).

75 On Eve, see Edwards (2012) and on Delilah, see Blyth (2017).

76 The man received God's instruction (Genesis 2:16) and was with Eve when she ate of the fruit (Genesis 3:6). Samson, meanwhile, ought to have known what Delilah was up to – given that he was subdued on Delilah's *fourth* attempt to find out the secret of his strength. Moreover, she asked him outright what the secret was – with no deception.

77 Jezebel does paint her eyes and adorn her head immediately prior to her death (2 Kings 9:30). This could signal an attempt at seduction but is more likely to signify her dignity (i.e. she is going into death looking regal). Her sexualization is clearer in the New Testament (Revelation 2:20–22). While Jezebel is not depicted in eroticized terms in the Hebrew Bible, this sexualization is likely to be due in no small part to her foreignness and the trope of the dangerously sexual 'foreign' woman, prominent throughout the Bible and into the present day (see Stiebert 2019: 85–92). The persistence of this interpretation of Jezebel right up to the present is clear in the depiction of the most marginalized of sex workers as Jezebels in the novel and television adaptation of Margaret Atwood's *The Handmaid's Tale*. The film *Jezebel* (1938) starring Bette Davis, which, according to its trailer, depicts a 'spitfire' of a woman with 'wild desires', demonstrates a similar set of connections. Understanding such associations of 'Jezebel' relies on widespread popular understanding of this character as 'sexual' and 'sinner' – an understanding based *not* on the biblical text but rather on its interpretation and reception.

78 Notably, two of these women are othered on account of their ethnicity and Delilah, while not identified as Philistine, collaborates with the Philistines. Jezebel is Phoenician and Potiphar's wife is Egyptian (see Note 77 above).

79 A careful distinction needs to be drawn between rape fantasy and rape. With rape fantasy a person remains in control; with rape, the victim's control is taken away. Fantasizing about rape is relatively common but is not the same as desiring rape. Having fantasies about rape does not justify rape or make it less traumatic (Zurbriggen and Yost 2004).

80 See Introduction, Note 4.

81 Just as rape victims' responses to rape are various and cannot be prescribed or scripted, nor can predilections in matters sexual. I am not denying that some persons enjoy so-called wild or even physically injurious sex. I am arguing, instead, that such sex, too, is bound by consent. But some rape myths compromise consent by promoting the idea that consent to rough sex, for instance, in one particular set of circumstances or with one particular person translates to a licence for rough sex in other circumstances, or with other persons, without the requirement for subsequent consent. Related to this are the rape myths that some persons, notably sex workers, or persons labelled 'loose' or 'sluts', are always available for sex, or rapable, that women enjoy being violently overpowered, and that sexual violence is, or can be, indicative of great passion. Such rape myths have acutely damaging consequences (see Moore and Khan 2019).

82 These articles report on cases from Spain, the USA, New Zealand, and England respectively. In all of them the defence makes recourse to the victim's alleged predilection for consenting BDSM (bondage, discipline/domination, submission/sadism, and masochism) or rough sex in order to dispute rape and (in two of the cases) murder.

83 The word 'complainant' is an unfortunate legal term pertaining to a plaintiff in certain lawsuits including in allegations of rape.

84 In another case from Spain, involving six men accused of sexual abuse of a 14-year-old girl, it was also disputed that this constituted gang-rape, on the grounds that the girl was drunk, under the influence of drugs, and did not fight back (Burgen 2019).

85 I have already mentioned that sex workers are not only very vulnerable to sexual violence and rape but also depicted as rapable. Again, the Bible reflects this rape myth. When Dinah's brothers justify their violent rampage of murder, kidnapping, and looting against the Hivites, they say to Jacob, their father, 'Should our sister be treated like a whore?' (Genesis 34:31, NRSV). The word translated 'whore' is Hebrew *zônâ*, which can refer to a woman who receives payment in return for sex (as is clearly suggested both in these verses from Ezekiel 16 and in Genesis 38:21–23). Given that the catalyst for the violence was their sister Dinah's rape by Shechem, a Hivite prince, the brothers' retort to Jacob suggests that rape is something that may be done to a sex worker – but not their sister. A sex worker, by implication, is rapable and has no honour to be salvaged; their honour is reclaimed through killing all Hivite males, taking back Dinah, plundering Hivite possessions, and seizing all women and girls (possibly for rape, though this is not stated explicitly).

86 Ezekiel 23 is similar. Here feminized Samaria and Jerusalem '[play] the whore' (Ezekiel 23:5) and practise 'whorings' (Ezekiel 23:11) with many foreign men who then, with God's assent, rape and brutalize them (Ezekiel 23:9–10, 22–29) (all quotations are from NRSV).

87 I agree with Friedman (2012: 377) that the text of Numbers 5 'does not reveal whether a woman's intercourse of seed was rape or consensual'.

Here, the woman suspected of adultery is by inference guilty. If a man other than her husband had sex with her (Numbers 5:20) rape is not considered as a possibility. Instead, if she had sex with another man she is an adulteress, never a rape victim, and must suffer pain and ostracism (Numbers 5:27).

88 This is confirmed by 2 Samuel 13. Amnon also seizes Tamar (v.11) and rapes her (v.14). Tamar tries to avert or postpone the rape by proposing marriage (v.13).

89 Rashkow, in her reading of Deuteronomy 22:13–21, hints at incestuous rape. She proposes that in this scenario, where a husband suspects his bride not to have been a virgin, it is the father who becomes defendant because '[i]mplicitly, the husband has accused the father, the man who gave him this woman, of having taken the husband's property (her virginity) in advance' (Rashkow 2000: 29).

90 Two different terms are used here. A *man* lies with a *male* 'the lyings of a woman'. What is possibly being prohibited here is penetrative sex between two males. The male who is lain with is not specifically an adult man (unlike the subject of the verb). Consequently, the prohibition could be condemning to death a boy-child, as well as any other male victim of rape.

91 Brafman, tapping into not inconsiderable public sentiment, asserts, 'If a woman has sex to help her Hollywood career, that is not rape' (Pavia 2018).

92 Greer's words were, 'If you spread your legs because [Weinstein] said "be nice to me and I'll give you a job in a movie" then I'm afraid that's tantamount to consent, and it's too late now to start whingeing about that' (Kaplan 2018). Greer's distillation of Weinstein's actions or actors' responses does not capture allegations very well (see Farrow 2017; Kantor and Twohey 2017).

93 This also applies to some of the responses to Christine Blasey Ford's plausible allegations of sexual assault against Brett Kavanaugh, made at the time of his nomination to the Supreme Court in July 2018. The assault was said to have happened decades earlier when both were teenagers. Blasey Ford, who passed a polygraph test and had discussed the assault in therapy sessions in 2012 and 2013, received praise and sympathy from some quarters and vitriol from others. Those who condemned her accused her of maliciously lying and seeking to ruin an innocent man, or of over-reacting to nothing more than teenage clumsiness.

94 See Chapter 1, Note 19.

95 For one of many articles calling out such discrepancy, see *The Independent* (2017). For an independent fact check, see Full Fact (2013). According to one source, false rape allegation is pursued with particularly harsh rigour in the UK (Laville 2014). On the Bible and false rape allegation in Genesis 39, see Notes 35 and 68 above and Stiebert (2019).

96 This is visually represented in the influential and commercially successful early film *The Birth of a Nation* (1915), which portrayed Black men as unintelligent and sexually aggressive towards white women. In the Nazi propaganda film *Jud Süß* (1940) the racist trope is adapted to Jewish Joseph Süß Oppenheimer who rapes the German maiden Dorothea. Both Elsie in the former and Dorothea in the latter film commit suicide, which exacerbates the sense of danger and horror posed by othered rapists. In a rally

addressing his supporters, Donald Trump also tapped into deep-rooted and persistent variants of the rapist as evil, dark 'other' by characterizing Mexican migrants as 'drug dealers, criminals, rapists' (see BBC News 2016).

97 Hence, Moses has a Cushite wife (Numbers 12:2). Miriam and Aaron challenge Moses about this wife but YHWH sides with Moses. While the unnamed Cushite wife is likely to have been Black-skinned (cf. Jeremiah 13:23), Miriam is punished with a skin disease that renders her white as snow (Numbers 12:10). Other revered figures also have non-Hebrew wives. Joseph's sons Manasseh and Ephraim, for example, have an Egyptian mother, Asenath (Genesis 41:50–52). A later, Hellenistic text, *Joseph and Aseneth*, turns Joseph's wife into a model proselyte. It seems this was necessary to make sense of an (otherwise not approved of) inter-ethnic union. Similarly, Ruth's Moabite ethnicity (mentioned multiple times in the short biblical book) is clearly a problem. Again, the book goes to great lengths to demonstrate that while a Moabite, Ruth is virtuous and 'worthy' of marriage to an Israelite. Racist ideology is thus pronounced in many biblical texts. This extends also to the New Testament, which contains anti-Jewish and anti-Samaritan sentiments (Patte 1988).

98 The incest laws of Leviticus 18 are prefaced with an inculcation not to do 'as they do in the land of Egypt … and … in the land of Canaan' (Leviticus 18:3), again linking sexual depravity and foreignness.

99 See above (pp. 68–69) on rape and marriage.

In conclusion

The Bible is a powerful and influential text: first, but not only, in the context of faith settings, where its words are held to be of divine origin. On account of its authority for Jews and Christians, the Bible continues to appear frequently as a prooftext. Easiest to identify here are examples from conservative Protestant traditions, such as those which defend Donald Trump or Brett Kavanaugh, for instance, with recourse to biblical figures such as King David or Joseph. But the Bible also has wider cultural power beyond faith settings and influences law, language, art, customs, values, mass protest movements, and popular culture.

Human communities have left traces *in* the extant biblical texts, which are detectable both in terms of what is said and how, as well as in what is unsaid, or assumed. In this way biblical texts contain markers of ideology, dominant attitudes, and social conflicts. Popular media and culture of the present, likewise, are marked by traces of the preoccupations, values, and social tensions of our time. The premise of this book is that gender relations and sexual violence are a shared preoccupation and locus of social conflict.

Just as texts – ancient and modern – are shaped by persons susceptible to their setting, so are interpretations of texts. I have argued here that meaning is created in and by settings and that it is, consequently, no accident that feminist biblical criticism, for instance, closely followed second-wave feminism. Feminist criticism, moreover, was instrumental in terms of shining a light on gendered violence in the Bible. In both Hebrew Bible and New Testament studies feminist critics were at the forefront of examining patterns of gender hierarchy and gender-based violence. And in examining biblical texts, feminist critics also reflected on misogyny, sexism, and violence against women in their own settings, as well as on the tensions and dynamics between texts, on the one hand, and actual women's experiences, on the other.

Biblical studies has, in many ways, remained traditional and rooted in the study of ancient languages, textual investigation, and historical criticism. But for a range of reasons there are also movements within the discipline – some of which have drawn from feminist advocacy – that are open to acknowledging the bearing of present events on interpretive processes. This book, following recent studies that have reflected on rape culture alongside biblical texts, draws on the impact of #MeToo to examine widespread sexualized violence. The focus on tools and strategies from traditional biblical studies – such as examination of key vocabulary in Biblical Hebrew and Koine Greek, close reading of primary texts, and consultation of academic secondary sources – is deliberately counter-pointed with sources responding to current events (reports, news sources, online material) to explore meaning-making and interpretation in the present.

#MeToo has been a highly visible and influential movement that has demonstrated the extent of rape culture. While rape cultures manifest in diverse ways, the term aptly describes human societies where sexual violence is underpinned by microaggressions and low-level sexism that bring about the downplaying of more serious forms of sexual violence. The consequence of this is that rape, while considered a serious crime, remains worryingly common. Another way that rape cultures are sustained is by the persistence of rape myths. These widely accepted but false beliefs serve to undermine rape victims and to embolden rape perpetrators.

For all the gains made by feminism, many toxic attitudes, including those pertaining to gender-based violence, which are already clearly marked in the Bible, still prevail. This is evident, too, in some of the backlash to #MeToo, which seeks to characterize the movement as a 'witchhunt' or a moral panic. #MeToo can be legitimately criticized for reinscribing patterns that continue to privilege some groups (i.e. wealthier, Western, white women) and marginalize the most vulnerable – such as members of Black and minority ethnic (BME), Two-Thirds world, and LGBTQ communities, as well as those with disabilities. What it has shown is that sexual harassment and abuse are rife – and if this is the case in more advantaged communities, then the situation in disadvantaged communities is even more alarming.

This demands action and careful dismantling of structures that support and perpetuate rape myths and rape cultures. Given the scale of the crisis, much change is required on many levels and in a range of sectors – among them legal, educational, and health sectors. One dimension of this, too, is to acknowledge the role and influence of religion, inclusive of the Bible. What this book has sought to do is to demonstrate, first, the abundance of material in the Bible that is indicative of rape-supportive attitudes; and, second, the prevailing influence and continuity of these attitudes in the present. Alongside this, I have tried to show that #MeToo has provided a strong impetus for calling out not only powerful and abusive individuals, but also powerful and abusive texts and interpretations. And this, I hope, is another step in the direction towards stemming and dismantling rape culture. While it may feel like a small step, it is clear to me that the most horrific of sexual crimes are built on edifices of other, including less invasive, actions and attitudes. It is, therefore, a step worth taking.

Bibliography

#SheToo podcast series. The Bible Society. Available online: www.bible society.org (accessed 16 May 2019).

11th Principle: Consent! Available online: www.11thprincipleconsent.org/consent-propaganda/rape-culture-pyramid/ (accessed 27 May 2019).

Adams, Carol J. 2005. '"I Just Raped My Wife! What Are You Going to Do about It, Pastor?": The Church and Sexual Violence'. In *Transforming A Rape Culture* (rev. edn). Edited by Emilie Buchwald, Pamela R. Fletcher, and Martha Roth. Minneapolis, MN: Milkweed Editions, pp. 75–104.

Afify, Heba. 5 January 2019. 'Egypt's #MeToo moment targets street harassment'. *CNN*. Available online: www.cnn.com/cnn/2019/01/04/health/egypt-sexual-harassment-intl/index.html (accessed 7 January 2019).

American Media Inc. (no author). 1 March 2018. 'Texas cheerleader's boyfriend charged with rape and murder after alleged "rough" sex'. *Ottawa Citizen*. Available online: https://ottawacitizen.com/news/crime/texas-cheerleaders-boyfriend-charged-with-rape-and-murder-after-alleged-rough-sex/wcm/058ad9fd-68e0-46bc-b774-5c7244f4b682 (accessed 6 July 2019).

Austin, Rod. 28 June 2019. 'Conflict drives global rise in sexual violence against women'. *Guardian*. Available online: www.theguardian.com/global-development/2019/jun/28/congo-abuses-drive-global-rise-in-sexual-violence-against-women (accessed 29 June 2019).

Bailey, Randall C. 2010. 'Why Do Readers Believe Lot? Genesis 19 Reconsidered'. *Old Testament Essays* 23/3: 519–48.

Bakare, Lanre. 10 May 2019. 'Cannes festival adapts to #MeToo era – but gender issues remain'. *Guardian*. Available online: www.theguardian.com/film/2019/may/10/cannes-festival-adapts-metoo-era-gender-issues-remain (accessed 12 May 2019).

Bal, Mieke. 1988. *Death and Dissymmetry: The Politics of Coherence in the Book of Judges*. Chicago, IL: University of Chicago Press.

Banet-Weiser, Sarah. 21 January 2015. 'Popular misogyny: A zeitgeist'. *Culture Digitally*. Available online: http://culturedigitally.org/2015/01/popular-misogyny-a-zeitgeist/ (accessed 25 April 2019).

Barber, Kathryn. 1 December 2018. 'UN 16 days of activism – Day 7: Kathryn Barber'. The Shiloh Project. Available online: https://shiloh-project.group.shef. ac.uk/un-16-days-of-activism-day-12-kathryn-barber/ (accessed 25 April 2019).

BBC News. 17 December 2018. 'Millionaire jailed for girlfriend's "rough sex" death'. Available online: www.bbc.com/news/uk-england-46591150 (accessed 6 July 2019).

BBC News. 25 April 2018. 'Elliot Rodger: How misogynist killer became "incel hero"'. Available online: www.bbc.com/news/amp/world-us-canada-43892189 (accessed 24 July 2019).

BBC News. 31 August 2016. '"Drug dealers, criminals, rapists": What Trump thinks of Mexicans'. Available online: www.bbc.co.uk/news/av/world-us-canada-37230916/drug-dealers-criminals-rapists-what-trump-thinks-of-mexicans (accessed 17 July 2019).

Bechtel, Lyn M. 1994. 'What if Dinah is not Raped? (Genesis 34)'. *Journal for the Study of the Old Testament* 62: 19–36.

Bible Hub. Available online: https://biblehub.com/ (accessed 12 December 2018).

Blenkinsopp, Joseph. 1997. 'The Family in First Temple Israel'. In *Families in Ancient Israel*. Edited by Leo G. Perdue, Joseph Blenkinsopp, John J. Collins, and Carol Meyers. Louisville, KY: Westminster John Knox, pp. 48–103.

Blyth, Caroline. 2017. *Reimagining Delilah's Afterlives as Femme Fatale: The Lost Seduction* (Library of Biblical Studies). London/New York: Bloomsbury T&T Clark.

Blyth, Caroline. 2010. *The Narrative of Rape in Genesis 34: Interpreting Dinah's Silence*. Oxford: Oxford University Press.

Blyth, Caroline, Emily Colgan, and Katie B. Edwards (eds.). 2018. *Rape Culture, Gender Violence, & Religion: Biblical Perspectives* (Religion and Radicalism). Cham, Switzerland: Palgrave Macmillan.

Bowcott, Owen. 2 April 2019. 'English judge says man having sex with wife is "fundamental human right"'. *Guardian*. Available online: www.theguardian. com/law/2019/apr/03/english-judge-says-man-having-sex-with-wife-is-fundamental-human-right (accessed 20 April 2019).

Brenner, Athalya. 1996. 'Pornoprophetics Revisited: Some Additional Reflections'. *Journal for the Study of the Old Testament* 70: 63–86.

Brittain, Amy, and Irin Carmon. 3 May 2018. 'Charlie Rose's misconduct was widespread at CBS and three managers were warned, investigation finds'. *Washington Post*. Available online: www.washingtonpost.com/charlie-roses-misconduct-was-widespread-at-cbs-and-three-managers-were-warned-investigation-finds/2018/05/02/80613d24-3228-11e8-94fa-32d48460b955_story.html?utm_term=.7fb99680bc03 (accessed 23 April 2019).

Brown, Mark. 30 May 2018. 'Germaine Greer calls for punishment for rape to be reduced'. *Guardian*. Available online: www.theguardian.com/books/2018/may/30/germaine-greer-calls-for-punishment-for-to-be-reduced (accessed 13 June 2019).

Brown, Roger, and Helen Carasso. 2013. *Everything for Sale? The Marketisation of UK Higher Education*. London: Routledge.

Brownmiller, Susan. 1975. *Against Our Will: Women, Men, and Rape*. New York: Bantam.

Buchwald, Emilie, Pamela R. Fletcher, and Martha Roth (eds.). 2005. *Transforming A Rape Culture* (rev. edn). Minneapolis, MN: Milkweed Editions.

Burgen, Stephen. 3 July 2019. 'Spain: prosecutors claim attack not rape as victim "did not fight back"'. *Guardian*. Available online: www.theguardian. com/world/2019/jul/03/trial-push-for-lesser-sexual-abuse-charge-as-victim-did-not-fight-back (accessed 6 July 2019).

Campbell, Bradley, and Jason Manning. 2018. *The Rise of Victimhood Culture: Microaggressions, Safe Spaces, and the New Culture Wars*. Cham, Switzerland: Palgrave Macmillan.

Carroll, Robert P. 2006 [1986]. *Jeremiah* (Volume 1). Sheffield, UK: Sheffield Phoenix Press.

Carroll, Robert P. 1997 [1991]. *Wolf in the Sheepfold: The Bible as Problematic for Theology*. London: SCM.

Casewell, Deborah. 30 November 2017. 'On vulnerability and victims: Does #MeToo perpetuate rape culture?'. The Shiloh Project. Available online: http://shiloh-project.group.shef.ac.uk/on-vulnerability-and-victims-does-metoo-perpetuate-rape-culture/ (accessed 23 April 2019).

Cheung, Helier. 6 August 2014. 'Surrogate babies: Where can you have them, and is it legal?' *BBC News*. Available online: www.bbc.co.uk/news/world-28679020 (accessed 18 January 2019).

Clines, David J. A. 22 August 2018. 'The Ubiquitous Language of Violence in the Hebrew Bible'. Paper presented at the Joint Meeting of Oudtestamentisch Werkgezelschap, Society for Old Testament Studies, and Old Testament Society of South Africa, Groningen, The Netherlands, 22–24 August 2018. Available online: http://Sheffield.academia.edu/DavidClines (accessed 5 September 2019).

Clines, David J. A. 2009 [1995]. *Interested Parties: The Ideology of Writers and Readers of the Hebrew Bible*. Sheffield, UK: Sheffield Phoenix Press.

Coaston, Jane. 26 March 2018. 'The "biblical" defense of Trump's affair with Stormy Daniels'. Available online: www.vox.com/platform/amp/policy-and-politics/2018/3/26/17164268/stormy-daniels-donald-trump-bible-christian (accessed 1 December 2018).

Cohen, Mari. 9 January 2012. 'Teen slang: Why the word "rape" should never be used casually'. *Huffington Post*. Available online: https://m.huffingtonpost. co.uk'etry'teen-slang-why-the-word-r_n_1194059?ec_carp=90475183 09117689808 (accessed 25 December 2018).

Colgan, Emily, and Caroline Blyth. 2018. 'Tough Conversations: Teaching Gender Violence in Aotearoa New Zealand'. In *Rape Culture, Gender Violence, & Religion: Biblical Perspectives*. Edited by Caroline Blyth, Emily Colgan, and Katie B. Edwards. Cham, Switzerland: Palgrave Macmillan, pp. 201–07.

Cook-Daniels, Loree. 2008. 'Female perpetrators and male victims of sexual abuse: Facts and resources'. *Forge*. Available online: https://forge-forward. org/wp-content/docs/female-perpetrators-and-male-victims-facts-and-resources.pdf (accessed 20 April 2019).

Cramb, Auslan. 19 November 2018. 'Mother of teenager who took her own life after rape trial "appalled" by girl's thong being used against her in Irish case'. *Telegraph*. Available online: www.telegraph.co.uk/news/2018/11/19/mother-teenager-took-life-rape-trial-appalled-girls-thong-used/ (accessed 16 February 2019).

Crenshaw, James L. 1984. *A Whirlpool of Torment*. Philadelphia, PA: Fortress Press.

Crenshaw, Kimberlé Williams. 1991. 'Mapping the Margins: Intersectionality, Identity Politics, and Violence against Women of Color'. *Stanford Law Review* 43/6: 1241–99.

Crown Prosecution Service. 2017. 'Rape and sexual offences – Chapter 19: Sentencing'. Available online: www.cps.gov.uk/legal-guidance/rape-and-sexual-offences-chapter-19-sentencing (accessed 5 September 2019).

Davies, Eryl W. 2003. *The Dissenting Reader: Feminist Approaches to the Hebrew Bible*. Aldershot, UK: Ashgate.

Davis, Angela Y. 1981. *Women, Race and Class*. New York: Random House.

Dube, Musa W. 2017. 'Dinah (Genesis 34) at the Contact Zone: "Shall Our Sister Become a Whore?"'. In *Feminist Frameworks and the Bible: Power, Ambiguity, and Intersectionality*. Edited by Juliana Claassens and Carolyn J. Sharp. London/New York: Bloomsbury T&T Clark, pp. 39–57.

Duff, Michelle. 25 May 2018. 'Is rough sex the new rape defence?' *Stuff*. Available online: www.stuff.co.nz/life-style/104216482/is-rough-sex-the-new-rape-defence (accessed 6 July 2019).

Dunbar, Ericka. 30 October 2018. 'For such a time as this? #UsToo: Sexual trafficking, silence, & secrecy in the Book of Esther'. The Shiloh Project. Available online: https://shiloh-project.group.shef.ac.uk/for-such-a-time-as-this-ustoo-sexual-trafficking-silence-secrecy-in-the-book-of-esther/ (accessed 18 December 2018).

Economist Intelligence Unit. 2019. 'Shining light on the response to child sexual abuse and exploitation'. World Childhood Foundation, Oak Foundation, and Carlson Family Foundation. Available online: http://outofthe shadows.eiu.com (accessed 9 May 2019).

Edwards, Katie. 2018. 'White is Purity: Christian Imagery, Popular Culture and the Construction of Whiteness'. In *The Bible, Centres and Margins: Dialogues Between Postcolonial African and British Biblical Scholars*. Edited by Johanna Stiebert and Musa W. Dube. London/New York: Bloomsbury T&T Clark, pp. 41–56.

Edwards, Katie (ed.). 2015. *Rethinking Biblical Literacy*. London/New York: Bloomsbury T&T Clark.

Edwards, Katie B. 2012. *Admen and Eve: The Bible in Contemporary Advertising* (The Bible in the Modern World, 48). Sheffield, UK: Phoenix.

Ellis-Petersen, Hannah. 17 January 2019. '"Time to start talking about consent": Thailand's nascent #MeToo moment'. *Guardian*. Available online: www.theguardian.com/world/2019/jan/17/time-to-start-talking-about-consent-thailands-nascent-metoo-moment (accessed 5 September 2019).

Exum, J. Cheryl. 2015 [1993]. *Fragmented Women: Feminist (Sub)versions of Biblical Narratives* (2nd edn). London: Bloomsbury T&T Clark.

Farrow, Ronan. 10 October 2017. 'From aggressive overtures to sexual assault: Harvey Weinstein's accusers tell their stories'. *The New Yorker*. Available online: www.newyorker.com/news/news-desk/from-aggressive-overtures-to-sexual-assault-harvey-weinsteins-accusers-tell-their-stories/amp (accessed 21 April 2019).

Fewell, Danna Nolan, and David L. Gunn. 1993. *Gender, Power, and Promise: The Story of the Bible's First Story*. Nashville, TN: Abingdon Press.

Filipovic, Jill. 2013. 'Rape is about power, not sex'. 29 August 2013. *Guardian*. Available online: www.theguardian.com/commentisfree/2013/aug/29/rape-about-power-not-sex (accessed 2 January 2019).

Fischer, Stefan. 2009. 'Die Machtstrukturen der Gewalt in Hoheslied'. *Protokolle zur Bibel* 18/2: 109–21.

Flood, Alison. 23 January 2018. 'Germaine Greer criticises "whingeing" #MeToo movement'. *Guardian*. Available online: www.theguardian.com/books/2018/jan/23/germaine-greer-criticises-whingeing-metoo-movement (accessed 13 July 2019).

Fortune, Marie M. 2005. 'Sexual Abuse by Religious Leaders'. In *Transforming A Rape Culture* (rev. edn). Edited by Emilie Buchwald, Pamela R. Fletcher, and Martha Roth. Minneapolis, MN: Milkweed Editions, pp. 189–200.

Friedman, Richard Elliott. 2012. 'The *Sotah*: Why Is This Case Different From All Other Cases?' In *Let Us Go Up to Zion: Essays in Honour of H. G. M. Williamson on the Occasion of his Sixty-Fifth Birthday* (Vetus Testamentum Supplements 153). Edited by Iain Provan and Mark Boda. Leiden: Brill, pp. 371–82.

Frymer-Kensky, Tikva. 1998. 'Virginity in the Bible'. In *Gender and Law in the Hebrew Bible and the Ancient Near East*. Edited by Victor H. Matthews, Bernard M. Levinson, and Tikva Frymer-Kensky. Sheffield, UK: Sheffield Academic Press, pp. 79–96.

Full Fact. 13 September 2013. 'False rape allegations: "serious, but rare"'. Available online: https://fullfact.org/crime/false-rape-allegations-serious-rare/ (accessed 27 April 2019).

Gaertner, Samuel L., John F. Dovidio, and Gary Johnson. 1982. 'Race of Victim, Nonresponsive Bystanders, and Helping Behavior'. *The Journal of Social Psychology* 117/1: 69–77.

Gafney, Wilda. 2009. 'Mother Knows Best: Messianic Surrogacy and Sexploitation in Ruth'. In *Mother Goose, Mother Jones, Mommie Dearest: Biblical Mothers and their Children*. Edited by Cheryl A. Kirk-Duggan and Tina Pippin. Atlanta, GA: Society of Biblical Literature, pp. 23–36.

Gay, Roxane (ed.). 2018. *Not That Bad: Dispatches from Rape Culture*. New York/London: Harper Perennial.

Gittos, Luke. 2015. *Why Rape Culture is a Dangerous Myth: From Steubenville to Ched Evans*. SOCIETAS Essays in Political and Cultural Criticism. Exeter, UK: Imprint Academic.

Glancy, Jennifer A., and Stephen D. Moore. 2011. 'How Typical a Roman Prostitute is Revelation's "Great Whore"?'. *Journal of Biblical Literature* 130/3: 551–69.

Government of the Republic of Botswana. 1998. 'Amended Laws'. Available online: www.gov.bw/en/Ministries-Authorities/Ministries/Ministry-of-Labour-Home-Affairs-MLHA/Gender-Issues/Amended-Laws-that-affected-the-status-of-women/?p_id=1437 (accessed 12 December 2018).

Gqola, Pumla Dineo. 2018 [2015]. *Rape: A South African Nightmare.* Auckland Park, South Africa: MFBooks Joburg.

Gravett, Sandie. 2004. 'Reading "Rape" in the Hebrew Bible: A Consideration of Language'. *Journal for the Study of the Old Testament* 28/3: 279–99.

Graybill, Rhiannon. (Forthcoming). 'Fuzzy, Messy, Icky: The Edges of Consent in Hebrew Bible Rape Narratives and Rape Culture'. *The Bible & Critical Theory* 15/2.

Graybill, Rhiannon. No date. 'Focus on teaching about sexual violence in the Hebrew Bible'. Oxford Biblical Studies Online. Available online: https://global.oup.obso/focus/focus_on_sexual_violence/ (accessed 16 May 2019).

Graybill, Rhiannon, Meredith Minister, and Beatrice Lawrence (eds.). 2019. *Rape Culture and Religious Studies: Critical and Pedagogical Engagements* (Feminist Studies and Sacred Texts). Lanham, MD: Lexington Books.

Greer, Germaine. 2018. *On Rape* (Little Books on Big Ideas). London/New York: Bloomsbury.

Griffiths, Rudyard (ed.). 2018. *Political Correctness Gone Mad?* (Dyson and Goldberg vs. Fry and Peterson, The Munk Debates). London: Oneworld Publications.

Guest, Deryn. 2011. 'From Gender Reversal to Genderfuck: Reading Jael Through a Lesbian Lens'. In *Bible Trouble: Queer Reading at the Boundaries of Biblical Scholarship.* Edited by Teresa J. Hornsby and Ken Stone. Atlanta, GA: Society of Biblical Literature, pp. 9–43.

Hall, Stuart. 1992. 'The West and the Rest: Discourse and Power'. In *Formations of Modernity.* Edited by Stuart Hall and Bram Gieben. Oxford: Polity, pp. 276–331.

Harding, Kate. 2015. *Asking For It: The Alarming Rise of Rape Culture – and What We Can Do About It.* Boston, MA: Da Capo Press.

Hargreaves, Frances. 20 November 2018. 'The #MeToo movement, intersectionality, and its implications for Dalit women'. The Shiloh Project. Available online: http://shiloh-project.group.shef.ac.uk/the-metoo-movement-intersectionality-and-its-implications-for-dalit-women/ (accessed 25 April 2019).

Hemery, Sophie, and Gayeti Singh. 4 May 2019. 'Feminist lawyers of South Asia rally to aid of #MeToo survivors'. *Guardian.* Available online: www.theguardian.com/world/2019/may/04/feminist-lawyers-south-asia-rally-to-support-of-metoo-survivors (accessed 5 May 2019).

Hengel, Martin. 1977. *Crucifixion: In the Ancient World and the Folly of the Message of the Cross.* Augsburg: Fortress Press.

Henley, Jon. 5 June 2019. 'Dutch girl was not "legally euthanised" and died at home'. *Guardian.* Available online: www.theguardian.com/world/2019/jun/05/noa-pothoven-netherlands-girl-not-legally-euthanised-died-at-home (accessed 15 June 2019).

Hill, Zahara. 18 October 2017. 'A Black woman created the "Me Too" campaign against sexual assault 10 years ago'. *Ebony*. Available online: www. ebony.com/news/black-woman-me-too-movement-tarana-burke-alyssa-milano#axzz4yxFYimkJ (accessed 1 December 2018).

Hirsch, Aubrey. 2018. 'Fragments'. In *Not That Bad: Dispatches from Rape Culture*. Edited by Roxane Gay. New York/London: Harper Perennial, pp. 1–13.

Hornsby, Teresa J. 2014. 'Heteronormativity/Heterosexism'. In *The Oxford Encyclopedia of the Bible and Gender Studies*, vol. 1. Edited by Julia M. O'Brien (ed. in chief). Oxford: Oxford University Press, pp. 321–27.

Hornsby, Teresa J., and Ken Stone (eds). 2011. *Bible Trouble: Queer Reading at the Boundaries of Biblical Scholarship*. Atlanta, GA: Society of Biblical Literature.

Independent. 25 August 2017. 'False rape allegations are rare – rape is not. Stop using the case of Jemma Beale to discredit all women'. Available online: www.independent.co.uk/voices/jemma-beale-woman-lie-about-rape-ten-years-in-prison-not-all-woman-liars-not-all-men-rapists-a7912766.html (accessed 28 April 2019).

Institut national de santé publique du Québec. No date. 'Media kit on sexual assault'. Available online: www.inspq.qc.ca/en/sexual-assault/understanding-sexual-assault/consequences (accessed 2 January 2019).

IVF Group Surrogacy Services. Available online: https://ivf-international.com/surrogacy-in-ukraine (accessed 18 January 2019).

Jameson, Fredric. 1981. *The Political Unconscious: Narrative as a Socially Symbolic Act*. London: Methuen.

Javaid, Aliraza. 2018. *Male Rape, Masculinities, and Sexualities: Understanding, Policing, and Overcoming Male Sexual Victimisation*. New York: Palgrave Macmillan.

Jennings, Theodore W. 2003. *The Man Jesus Loved: Homoerotic Narratives from the New Testament*. Cleveland, OH: Pilgrim Press.

Jennings, Theodore W., and Tat-Siong Benny Liew. 2004. 'Mistaken Identities but Model Faith: Rereading the Centurion, the Chap, and the Christ in Matthew 8:5–13'. *Journal of Biblical Literature* 123/3: 467–94.

Jezebel. 1938. [A film directed by William Wyler]. Warner Bros.

Jones, Sam. 5 December 2018. 'Spanish "Wolf Pack" verdict upheld, prompting fresh protests'. *Guardian*. Available online: www.theguardian.com/world/2018/dec/05/spain-court-upholds-wolf-pack-verdict-of-sexual-abuse-rather-than-rape-pamplona (accessed 15 February 2019).

Joseph and the Amazing Technicolor Dreamcoat. 1999. [A film directed by David Mallet and produced by Andrew Lloyd Webber, Andy Picheta, Nigel Wright, and Austin Shaw]. PolyGram Video.

Jud Süß. 1940. [A film directed by Veit Harlan and produced by Otto Lehmann]. Terra Film.

Kaiser, Anna Jean. 23 December 2018. 'Woman who Bolsonaro insulted: "Our president-elect encourages rape"'. *Guardian*. Available online: www.theguardian.com/world/2018/dec/23/maria-do-rosario-jair-bolsonaro-brazil-rape (accessed 14 June 2019).

Kale, Sirin. 6 May 2016. 'Why a court may not believe you were raped if you're into rough sex'. *Vice.* Available online: www.vice.com/en_us/article/gvz43y/why-a-court-may-not-believe-you-were-raped-if-youre-into-rough-sex (accessed 6 July 2019).

Kalmanofsky, Amy. 2017. 'How Feminist Biblical Scholarship Can Heal Victims of Sexual Violation'. In *Sexual Violence and Sacred Texts.* Edited by Amy Kalmanofsky. Cambridge, MA: Feminist Studies in Religion Books, pp. 9–30.

Kantor, Jodi, and Megan Twohey. 5 October 2017. 'Harvey Weinstein paid off sexual harassment accusers for decades'. *New York Times.* Available online: www.nytimes.com/2017/10/05/us/harvey-weinstein-harassment-allegations.amp.html (accessed 21 April 2019).

Kaplan, Ilana. 22 January 2018. 'Germaine Greer says women "spread legs" for Weinstein movie roles'. *Independent.* Available online: www.independent.co.uk/arts-entertainment/germaine-greer-me-too-harvey-weinstein-women-spread-legs-movie-roles-actress-a8173161.html%3famp (accessed 11 July 2019).

Kawashima, Robert. 2011. 'Could A Woman Say "No" in Biblical Israel? On the Genealogy of Legal Status in Biblical Law and Literature'. *Association for Jewish Studies Review* 35: 1–22.

Keady, Jessica. 2018. 'Rape Culture Discourse and Female Impurity: Genesis 34 as a Case Study'. In *Rape Culture, Gender Violence, & Religion: Biblical Perspectives.* Edited by Caroline Blyth, Emily Colgan, and Katie B. Edwards. Cham, Switzerland: Palgrave Macmillan, pp. 67–82.

Keefe, Alice A. 1993. 'Rapes of Women, Wars of Men: Women, War, Society, and Metaphoric Language in the Study of the Hebrew Bible'. *Semeia* 61 (Women, War, and Metaphor): 79–97.

Kennedy, Maev. 29 September 2009. 'Polanski was not guilty of "rape-rape"', says Whoopi Goldberg'. *Guardian.* Available online: www.theguardian.com/film/2009/sep/29/roman-polanski-whoopi-goldberg (accessed 13 June 2019).

Kennelly, Larissa, and Mohamed Madi. 16 January 2018. 'Rape survivors' clothing on display'. *BBC News.* Available online: www.bbc.co.uk'news/av/world-europe-42668362/rape-survivors-clothing-on-display (accessed 14 June 2019).

Kilpatrick, Dean G., Patricia A. Resick, and Lois J. Veronen. 1981. 'Effects of a Rape Experience: A Longitudinal Study'. *Journal of Social Issues* 37/4: 105–22.

Kinloch, Valerie. 2006. *June Jordan: Her Life and Letters* (Women Writers of Color). Westport, CT: Praeger.

Klopper, Frances. 2010. 'Rape and the Case of Dinah: Ethical Responsibilities for Reading Genesis 34'. *Old Testament Essays* 23/3: 652–65.

Krishnan, Murali. 26 June 2018. 'Is India the worst place in the world to be a woman?' *DW.COM.* Available online: www.dw.com/en/is-india-the-worst-place-in-the-world-to-be-a-woman/a-44406279 (accessed 13 June 2019).

Kügler, Joachim. 2017. 'Josef, David und andere schöne Männer in der Bibel: Männliche Schönheit als Gottesmacht'. Available online: www.academia.edu/35471659 (accessed 14 March 2019).

Lartey, Jamiles. 23 March 2019. 'Barbra Streisand apologises for comments on Michael Jackson's accusers'. *Guardian*. Available online: www.theguardian.com/culture/2019/mar/23/michael-jackson-barbra-streisand-leaving-neverland (accessed 5 July 2019).

Laville, Sandra. 1 December 2014. '109 women prosecuted for false rape claims in five years, say campaigners'. *Guardian*. Available online: www.theguardian.com/law/2014/dec/01/109-women-prosecuted-false-rape-allegations (accessed 27 April 2018).

Lipsett, Anthea. 5 March 2009. 'Arts and language subjects miss out on funding'. *Guardian*. Available online: www.theguardian.com/education/2009/mar/05/universityfunding-researchfunding (accessed 16 May 2019).

Lloyd-Roberts, Sue and Sarah Morris. 2016. *The War on Women: And the Brave Ones Who Fight Back*. London/New York: Simon & Schuster.

Lombard, Nancy (ed.). 2018. *The Routledge Handbook of Gender and Violence*. New York: Routledge.

Marchal, Joseph A. 2011. 'The Usefulness of an Onesimus: The Sexual Use of Slaves and Paul's Letter to Philemon'. *Journal of Biblical Literature* 130/4: 749–70.

Marshall, John W. 2009. 'Gender and Empire: Sexualized Violence in John's Anti-Imperial Apocalypse'. In *A Feminist Companion to the Apocalypse of John*. Edited by Amy-Jill Levine, with Maria Mayo Robbins. London: T&T Clark, pp. 17–32.

Matthews, Shelly. 2017. ' "To Be One and the Same with the Woman Whose Head Is Shaven": Resisting the Violence of 1 Corinthians 11:2–16 from the Bottom of the Kyriarchal Pyramid'. In *Sexual Violence and Sacred Texts*. Edited by Amy Kalmanofsky. Cambridge, MA: Feminist Studies in Religion Books, pp. 31–51.

Matthews, Shelly. No date. 'Violence in the New Testament'. Available online: www.bibleodyssey.org/en/passages/related-articles/violence-in-the-new-testament (accessed on 7 December 2018).

McKeating, Henry. 1979. 'Sanctions Against Adultery in Ancient Israelite Society, with Some Reflections on Methodology in the Study of Old Testament Ethics'. *Journal for the Study of the Old Testament* 11: 57–72.

Mendes, Kaitlynn, Jessica Ringrose, and Jessalynn Keller. 2019. *Digital Feminist Activism: Girls and Women Fight Back Against Rape Culture* (Oxford Studies in Digital Politics). Oxford: Oxford University Press.

Minister, Meredith. 2018. *Rape Culture on Campus*. Lanham, MD: Lexington Books.

Ministry of Justice, Home Office, and the Office for National Statistics. 2013. 'An overview of sexual offending in England and Wales'. Available online: https://assets.publishing.service.gov.uk/government/uploads/system/uploads/attachment_data/file/214970/sexual-offending-overview-jan-2013.pdf (accessed 6 September 2019).

Moore, Anna, and Coco Khan. 25 July 2019. 'The fatal, hateful rise of choking during sex'. *Guardian*. Available online: www.theguardian.com/society/2019/jul/25/fatal-hateful-rise-of-choking-during-sex (accessed 27 July 2019).

Morales, Mark. 4 January 2019. '#MeToo cited as one reason rape reports increased 22% in New York in 2018'. *CNN*. Available online: https://edition.cnn.com/2019/01/03/us/nypd-crime-stats-briefing/index.html (accessed 5 January 2019).

Moyo, Fulata Lusungu. 2017. 'Gang-Raped and Dis-Membered: Contextual Biblical Study of Judges 19:1–30 to Re-Member the Rwandan Genocide'. In *Sexual Violence and Sacred Texts*. Edited by Amy Kalmanofsky. Indianapolis, IN: Dog Ear Publishing, pp. 125–39.

Mulvihill, Natasha. 2018. 'Prostitution and Violence'. In *The Routledge Handbook of Gender and Violence*. Edited by Nancy Lombard. New York: Routledge, pp. 223–34.

Nagouse, Emma. 2018. ' "To Ransom a Man's Soul": Male Rape and Gender Identity in Outlander and "The Suffering Man" of Lamentations 3'. In *Rape Culture, Gender Violence, & Religion: Biblical Perspectives*. Edited by Caroline Blyth, Emily Colgan, and Katie B. Edwards. Cham, Switzerland: Palgrave Macmillan, pp. 143–58.

Nwaubani, Adaobi Tricia. 20 December 2018. 'The women rescued from Boko Haram who are returning to their captors'. *The New Yorker*. Available online: www.newyorker.com/news/dispatch/the-women-rescued-from-boko-haram-who-are-returning-to-their-captors/amp (accessed 15 July 2019).

Office for National Statistics. 2018. 'Sexual offences in England and Wales: Year ending March 2017'. Available online: www.ons.gov.uk/people populationandcommunity/crimeandjustice/articles/sexualoffencesinengland andwales/yearendingmarch2017 (accessed 7 January 2019).

Patte, Daniel. 1988. 'Anti-Semitism in the New Testament: Confronting the Dark Side of Paul's and Matthew's Teaching'. *Chicago Theological Seminary Register* 78/1: 31–52.

Pavia, Will. 3 March 2018. 'Saturday interview: Benjamin Brafman'. *The Times*. Available online: www.thetimes.co.uk/article/benjamin-brafman-interview-if-a-woman-has-sex-to-help-her-hollywood-career-that-is-not-rape-cdcz2rl6p?utm_source=FBPAGE&utm_medium=social_ Unspecified&UTMX=:The%20Times%20&%20The%20Sunday%20 Times:Unspecified:Unspecified (accessed 7 January 2019).

Penner, Todd, and Lilian Cates. 2007. 'Textually Violating Dinah: Literary Readings, Colonizing Interpretations, and the Pleasure of the Text'. *The Bible and Critical Theory* 3/3: 37.1–37.18.

Perraudin, Frances. 17 May 2019. 'Survey finds 70% of LGBT people sexually harassed at work'. *Guardian*. Available online: www.theguardian.com/uk-news/2019/may/17/survey-finds-70-of-lgbt-people-sexually-harassed-at-work (accessed 17 May 2019).

Peters, Michael A., and Tina Besley. 2019. 'Weinstein, Sexual Predation, and "Rape Culture": Public Pedagogies and Hashtag Internet Activism'. *Educational Philosophy and Theory* 51/5: 458–64.

Phillips, Melanie. 27 March 2018. 'Feminists are set on making us all victims'. *The Times*. Available online: www.thetimes.co.uk/edition/comment/feminists-are-set-on-making-us-all-victims-5vn9tkvvv (accessed 23 April 2019).

Phillips, Nickie D. 2017. *Beyond Blurred Lines: Rape Culture in Popular Media.* Lanham, MD: Rowman & Littlefield.

Phipps, Alison. 2009. 'Rape and Respectability: Ideas About Sexual Violence and Social Class'. *Sociology* 43/4: 667–83.

Phipps, Alison. Forthcoming. '"Every Woman Knows a Weinstein": Political Whiteness and White Woundedness in #MeToo and Public Feminism Around Sexual Violence'. *Feminist Formations* (volume and issue TBC). Available online: http://sro.sussex.ac.uk/id/eprint/83531/ (accessed 9 September 2019).

Pippin, Tina. 1996. 'Ideology, Ideological Criticism, and the Bible'. *Currents in Research: Biblical Studies* 4: 51–78.

Popova, Milena. 2019. *Sexual Consent* (MIT Press Essential Knowledge series). Cambridge, MA/London: The MIT Press.

Quackenbush, Casey. 22 November 2017. 'The religious community is speaking out against sexual violence with #ChurchToo'. *Time.* Available online: www.time.com/5034546/me-too-church-too-sexual-abuse/ (accessed 16 May 2019).

RAINN (Rape, Abuse & Incest National Network). 6 March 2014. 'Campus public policy: RAINN urges White House task force to overhaul colleges' treatment of rape'. Available online: www.rainn.org/news/rainn-urges-white-house-task-force-overhaul-colleges'-treatment-rape (accessed 14 June 2019).

RAINN (Rape, Abuse & Incest National Network). No date. 'Key terms and phrases'. Available online: www.rainn.org/articles/key-terms-and-phrases (accessed 7 January 2019).

Rape Crisis England & Wales. No date. 'Rape Crisis England & Wales headline statistics 2017-18'. Available online: https://rapecrisis.org.uk/get-informed/rcew-statistics/ (accessed 7 January 2019).

Rape Culture. 1975. [A film produced by Margaret Lazarus and Renner Wunderlich]. Cambridge Documentary Films.

Rashkow, Ilona N. 2000. 'Daughters and Fathers in Genesis … Or, What is Wrong with This Picture?'. In *A Feminist Companion to the Bible: Exodus to Deuteronomy* (2nd edn). Edited by Athalya Brenner. Sheffield, UK: Sheffield Academic Press, pp. 22–36.

Reis, Pamela Tamarkin. 1998. 'Cupidity and Stupidity: Women's Agency and the "Rape" of Tamar'. *Journal of the Ancient Near Eastern Society* 25: 43–60.

Rey, M. I. 2016. 'Reexamination of the Foreign Female Captive: Deuteronomy 21:10– 14 as a Case of Genocidal Rape'. *Journal of Feminist Studies in Religion* 32/1: 37–53.

Richardson, Hannah. 26 October 2010. 'Humanities to lose English universities teaching grant'. *BBC News.* Available online: www.bbc.co.uk/news/education-11627843 (accessed 16 May 2019).

Rodriguez, Damary. 8 November 2018. 'Centering trans survivors in the #MeToo movement'. Available online: www.nsvrc.org/blogs/centering-trans-survivors-metoo-movement (accessed 1 December 2018).

Rosell, Victoria. 26 June 2018. 'The "wolf pack" case showed the world how Spanish law is mired in misogyny'. *Guardian*. Available online: www.the guardian.com/commentisfree/2018/jun/26/wolf-pack-case-spain-law-misogyny (accessed 15 February 2019).

Sacco, Lynn. 2009. *Unspeakable: Father–Daughter Incest in American History*. Baltimore, MD: The Johns Hopkins University Press.

Sanday, Peggy Reeves. 2003. 'Rape-Free versus Rape-Prone: How Culture Makes a Difference'. In *Evolution, Gender, and Rape*. Edited by Cheryl Brown Travis. Cambridge, MA: MIT Press, pp. 337–62.

Sanyal, Mithu. 2019. *Rape: From Lucretia to #MeToo*. London/New York: Verso.

Scholz, Susanne. 2000. *Rape Plots: A Feminist Cultural Study of Genesis 34* (Studies in Biblical Literature, 13). New York: Peter Lang.

Scholz, Susanne. 2005. '"Back Then It Was Legal" The Epistemological Imbalance in Readings of Biblical and Ancient Near Eastern Rape Legislation'. *The Bible and Critical Theory* 1/4: 36.1–36.22. doi: 10.21o4/bc050036.

Scholz, Susanne. 2010. *Sacred Witness: Rape in the Hebrew Bible*, Minneapolis, MN: Fortress Press.

Scholz, Susanne. 2018. 'Marriage, Love, or Consensual Sex? Feminist Engagements with Biblical Rape Texts in Light of Title IX'. In *Rape Culture, Gender Violence, & Religion: Biblical Perspectives*. Edited by Caroline Blyth, Emily Colgan, and Katie B. Edwards. Cham, Switzerland: Palgrave Macmillan, pp. 179–99.

Schroeder, Joy A. 2007. *Dinah's Lament: The Biblical Legacy of Sexual Violence in Christian Interpretation*. Minneapolis, MN: Fortress Press.

Schulte, Leah Rediger. 2017. *The Absence of God in Biblical Rape Narratives*. Minneapolis, MN: Fortress Press.

Schüssler Fiorenza, Elisabeth. 2011. *Transforming Vision: Explorations in Feminist The*logy*. Minneapolis, MN: Fortress Press.

Sefaria. Available online: www.sefaria.org/ (accessed 26 December 2018).

Sen, Purna. 6 July 2018. 'Women are uniting against sexual violence – and we won't be stopped'. *Guardian*. Available online: www.theguardian.com/global-development/2018/jul/06/women-sexual-violence-harassment (accessed 29 June 2019).

Serisier, Tanya. January 2017. 'Sex Crimes and the Media'. Oxford Research Encyclopedia of Criminology and Criminal Justice. doi: 10.1093/acrefore/9780190264079.013.118.

Sexual Offences Act 2003. UK Government. Available online: www.legislation.gov.uk/ukpga/2003/42/part/1/crossheading/rape (accessed 12 December 2018).

Shackelford, Ashleigh. 21 September 2016. 'Society (and my rapist) says I'm too ugly to be raped'. Available online: http://ashleighshackelford.com/articles/2016/9/21/society-and-my-rapist-says-im-too-ugly-to-be-raped (accessed 14 June 2019).

Shaw, Danny. 10 March 2017. 'Retiring Judge Lindsey Kushner issues drunk women rape warning'. *BBC News*. Available online: www.bbc.co.uk/news/amp/uk-england-manchester-39233617 (accessed 14 June 2019).

Shemesh, Yael. 2007. 'Rape is Rape is Rape: The Story of Dinah and Shechem (Genesis 34)'. *Zeitschrift für die alttestamentliche Wissenschaft* 119/1: 2–21.

Sjoberg, Laura. 2016. *Women As Wartime Rapists: Beyond Sensation and Stereotyping*. New York: New York University Press.

Skrimshire, Stefan. 12 May 2019. 'Extinction Rebellion and the new visibility of religious protest'. *Open Democracy*. Available online: www.opendemocracy. net/en/transformation/extinction-rebellion-and-new-visibility-religious-protest/ (accessed 19 May 2019).

Squires, Nick. 24 October 2011. 'Vatican sides with anti-capitalist protesters and attacks global financial system'. *Telegraph*. Available online: www.telegraph. co.uk/finance/financialcrisis/8846595/Vatican-sides-with-anti-capitalist-protesters-and-attacks-global-financial-system.html (accessed 19 May 2019).

Stiebert, Johanna. 2013. *Fathers and Daughters in the Hebrew Bible*. Oxford: Oxford University Press.

Stiebert, Johanna. 2016. *First-Degree Incest and the Hebrew Bible: Sex in the Family* (Library of Hebrew Bible/Old Testament Studies, 596). New York: Bloomsbury T&T Clark.

Stiebert, Johanna. 2018. 'Denying Rape Culture: A Response to Luke Gittos'. *Women's Studies Journal* 32/1–2: 62–71. Available online: www.wsanz.org. nz/journal/docs/WSJNZ32Stiebert63-72.pdf (accessed 5 September 2019).

Stiebert, Johanna. 2019. 'The Wife of Potiphar, Sexual Harassment, and False Rape Allegation: Genesis 39 in Select Social Contexts of the Past and Present'. *Bible in Africa Studies* 22 (The Bible and Gender Troubles in Africa): 73–114.

Stiebert, Johanna. 27 September 2017. 'Rape culture denial: A response'. The Shiloh Project. Available online: https://shiloh-project.group.shef.ac.uk/ rape-culture-denial-a-response/ (accessed 5 January 2019).

Stone, Ken. 1996. *Sex, Honor, and Power in the Deuteronomistic History* (Journal for the Study of the Old Testament Supplement, 234). Sheffield, UK: Sheffield Academic Press.

Stone, Ken. 2007. ' "You Seduced Me, You Overpowered Me, and You Prevailed": Religious Experience and Homoerotic Sadomasochism in Jeremiah'. In *Patriarchs, Prophets and Other Villains*. Edited by Lisa Isherwood. London: Equinox, pp. 101–09.

Stone, Michael. 3 October 2018. 'Christians use Bible to defend Kavanaugh and discredit sexual assault survivors'. Available online: www.patheos.com/ blogs/progressivesecularhumanist/2018/10/Christians-use-bible-to-defend-kavanaugh-and-discredit-sexual-assault-survivors (accessed 7 January 2019).

Sugirtharajah, R. S. (ed.). 2008. *Still at the Margins: Biblical Scholarship Fifteen Years after the Voices from the Margin*. London/New York: Bloomsbury T&T Clark.

Suri, Manveena. 18 October 2018. 'India's #MeToo moment? Media and entertainment industry shaken by allegations'. *CNN*. Available online: https://edition.cnn.com/2018/10/10/asia/india-metoo-intl/index.html (accessed 23 October 2018).

Tamar Campaign. 2007. 'Contextual Bible study manual on gender-based violence'. Available online: http://sidebysidegender.org/wp-content/uploads/

2015/12/GBV-Tamar-Campaign-Contextual-Bible-Study-Manual-English-Version.pdf (accessed 18 January 2019).

Telegraph. 10 March 2019. 'Sir Cliff Richard backs pressure group pushing for anonymity for those accused of sexual offences'. Available online: www. telegraph.co.uk/news/2019/03/10/sir-cliff-richard-backs-pressure-group-pushing-anonymity-accused/amp/ (accessed 11 March 2019).

The Birth of a Nation. 1915. [A film directed by D. W. Griffith]. David W. Griffith Corp.

The Hunting Ground. 2015. [A film directed by Kirby Dick and produced by Amy Ziering]. The Weinstein Company.

The Shiloh Project. Available online: http://shiloh-project.group.shef.ac.uk (accessed 16 May 2019).

Thistlewaite, Susan Brooks. 1993. '"You May Enjoy the Spoil of Your Enemies": Rape as a Biblical Metaphor for War'. *Semeia* 61 (Women, War, and Metaphor): 59–78.

Thomson Reuters Foundation. 2018. 'The world's most dangerous countries for women (poll 2018)'. Available online: http://poll2018.trust.org (accessed 25 April 2019).

Tillet, Salamishah and Scheherazade Tillet. 10 January 2019. 'After the "Surviving R. Kelly" documentary, #MeToo has finally returned to Black girls'. *New York Times.* Available online: www.nytimes.com/2019/01/10/opinion/r-kelly-documentary-metoo.amp.html (accessed 1 June 2019).

Tombs, David. 1999. 'Crucifixion, State Terror and Sexual Abuse'. *Union Seminary Quarterly Review* 53: 89–109.

Topping, Alexandra, Kate Lyons, and Matthew Weaver. 15 January 2019. 'Gillette #MeToo razors ad on "toxic masculinity" gets praise – and abuse'. *Guardian.* Available online: www.theguardian.com/world/2019/jan/15/gillette-metoo-ad-on-toxic-masculinity-cuts-deep-with-mens-rights-activists (accessed 21 April 2019).

Trible, Phyllis. 1984. *Texts of Terror: Literary-Feminist Readings of Biblical Narratives* (Overtures to Biblical Theology). Philadelphia, PA: Fortress Press.

Ullendorff, Edward. 1978. *The Bawdy Bible.* Oxford: Oxford Centre for Postgraduate Studies.

van Dijk-Hemmes, Fokkelien. 1995. 'The Metaphorization of Woman in Prophetic Speech: An Analysis of Ezekiel 23'. In *A Feminist Companion to the Latter Prophets* (A Feminist Companion to the Bible, 8). Edited by Athalya Brenner. Sheffield, UK: Sheffield Academic Press, pp. 244–55.

Van Wolde, Ellen. 2002a. 'Does *'innâ* Denote Rape? A Semantic Analysis of a Controversial Word'. *Vetus Testamentum* 52/4: 528–44.

Van Wolde, Ellen. 2002b. 'The Dinah Story: Rape or Worse?' *Old Testament Essays* 15/1: 225–39.

Veselka, Vanessa. 1998. 'The collapsible woman: Cultural response to rape and abuse'. *BitchMedia.* Available online: www.bitchmedia.org/article/the-collapsible-woman (accessed 15 June 2019).

Wakefield, Jane. 29 November 2018. 'MeToo founder Tarana Burke: Campaign now "unrecognisable"'. *BBC*. Available online: www.bbc.co.uk/news/world-46393369 (accessed 7 January 2019).

Washington, Harold C. 1998. '"Lest He Die in Battle and Another Man Take Her": Violence and the Construction of Gender in the Laws of Deuteronomy 20–22'. In *Gender and Law in the Hebrew Bible and the Ancient Near East*. Edited by Victor H. Matthews, Bernard M. Levinson, and Tikva Frymer-Kensky. Sheffield, UK: Sheffield Academic Press, pp. 185–213.

Weems, Renita J. 1995. *Battered Love: Marriage, Sex, and Violence in the Hebrew Prophets*. Minneapolis, MN: Fortress Press.

Weems, Renita J. 1988. *Just a Sister Away: A Womanist Vision of Women's Relationships in the Bible*. San Diego, CA: LuraMedia.

Williams, Craig A. 1999. *Roman Homosexuality: Ideologies of Masculinity in Classical Antiquity* (Ideologies of Desire). Oxford: Oxford University Press.

Williams, Zoe. 15 January 2019. 'Does the age of consent push people to have sex too soon?' *Guardian*. Available online: www.theguardian.com/lifeandstyle/2019/jan/15/does-the-age-of-consent-push-people-to-have-sex-too-soon (accessed 21 April 2019).

Willsher, Kim. 1 June 2019. 'Moi aussi? Conflicted France at last tackles sexual harassment'. *Guardian*. Available online: www.theguardian.com/world/2019/jun/01/france-sex-abuse-police-chatline-me-too (accessed 2 June 2019).

Yamada, Frank M. 2008. *Configurations of Rape in the Hebrew Bible: A Literary Analysis of Three Rape Narratives*. New York: Peter Lang.

Zeichmann, Christopher B. 29 January 2018. 'A centurion and his "lover": A text of queer terror'. The Shiloh Project. Available online: https://shiloh-project.group.shef.ac.uk/a-centurion-and-his-lover-a-text-of-queer-terror/ (accessed 7 January 2019).

Zurbriggen, E. L., and M. R. Yost. 2004. 'Power, Desire, and Pleasure in Sexual Fantasies'. *Journal of Sex Research* 41/3: 288–300.

Zurcher, Anthony. 25 June 2019. 'Trump says sexual assault accuser E Jean Carroll "not my type"'. *BBC News*. Available online: www.bbc.com/news/amp/world-us-canada-48754959 (accessed 5 July 2019).

Index of authors and subjects

Index of biblical passages